**Here's what leaders like you
have already discovered in**

Re-Ignite Your Business!
The Secret of
Leading with Confidence,
Ease and Certainty

"This book makes accessible some truly profound concepts and strategies. It is a planning retreat, counseling session and executive consultation all compressed into an easy two hour read."

JIM CATHCART, Author
Relationship Selling and *The Acorn Principle*
The Cathcart Institute, La Jolla, CA
Mission: "Stimulating Abundance"

• • •

"Hey! You talk about going right to the core of why businesses go belly-up? Well...get this book...study it...and you'll never find you or your company out of the ball game! Never!"

ARNOLD "NICK" CARTER, Vice President
Nightingale-Conant, Niles, IL

• • •

"Getting focused is the key to just about anything. Here's the blueprint."

DIANNA BOOHER, Author
Get a Life Without Sacrificing Your Career
and *Communicate with Confidence*
Booher Consultants, Inc., Euless, TX

• • •

"I couldn't put this book down until I finished it! Every time I pick it up, I find more insight and inspiration. It has allowed me to become a leader of people – not just the manager of my own life."

REX EADS, CEO
Cascade Software Consulting, Vancouver, WA
Mission: "Everybody Wins"

• • •

"This is a great book! It's a quick, easy read – and it made things really click for me. I started reading it on a flight home after a long intense day of meetings. Before I was halfway through it – on page 41 to be exact – I was already reenergized, clear for the first time on my company's mission, and immediately generating ideas on how to put my new-found clarity into action in a team off-site. It worked!"

VICKY HASTINGS, Principal
The Hastings Company, Portland, OR
Mission: "Market Leadership"

• • •

"What a great little book! I'm sure that thousands of business leaders will pull this out of their briefcase on a flight home, and it will transform their approach to running their business."

ROGER DAWSON, Author
Roger Dawson's Secrets of Power Negotiation
City of Industry, CA

• • •

"Dick Barnett's work reads like a novel. It's content is a Bible. And he is a solid gold resource!"

TY BOYD, CSP, CPAE, Past President, NSA
Ty Boyd Training & Development, Inc.,
Charlotte, NC

• • •

"What a delight and honor to read how many of my ideas are being put into practice by a wise and effective consultant. His writing style is fresh, challenging and inspiring. I look forward to giving it to my consulting customers."

ROBERT W. TERRY, Author
Authentic Leadership: Courage in Action
The Terry Group, St. Paul, MN

• • •

"Recently I had the pleasure of reading Re-Ignite Your Business! *I was reading it with the intention of applying this to our business directly. To my surprise, not only has it been a real benefit in my work, it has "re-ignited" my family as well. The context can be applied in every aspect of life. It has truly made my mission of a happy family easy to fulfill. Thanks for giving me the opportunity to lift unnecessary burdens in my business and family life."*

JULIE UHOUSE, Customer Service
Wells Fargo Bank, Sacramento, CA
Mission: "Happy Family"

• • •

"As a student of leadership development, I'm always interested in new ideas and fresh perspectives. That's why I enjoyed this book. It is a rare combination: an easy read that is mentally stimulating. Although it won't take long to read, the ideas you encounter here stay with you for a long time."

MARK SANBORN, CSP, CPAE
Sanborn & Associates, Inc.,
Denver, CO

• • •

"Working through the current health care crisis, I don't think our hospital would have survived the last two years if we hadn't applied the concepts Dick develops in this book. Our mission led us powerfully and effectively...regardless of the circumstances we encountered.

MARY ANN BARNES, Hospital Administrator
Kaiser Permanente, Harbor City, CA
Mission: "Healthy Member"

• • •

"This book gives you the secrets of leading any business in the new millennium. Re-Ignite your attitude and buy this book!"

KEITH HARRELL, Author
Attitude is Everything
Harrell Performance Group, Inc., Atlanta, GA

• • •

"If you're looking for a tool to help you or your company win, You've just found it. Today's CEOs and management teams need solid coaching and a winning strategy that's applicable and doable in today's real business world. Re-Ignite Your Business! is loaded with workable wisdom. It's real, practical, and it will benefit you and your company. Enjoy it and succeed."

RAY PELLETIER,
America's Business Attitude Coach and Author
Permission To Win
The Pelletier Group, Miami Lakes, FL

• • •

"Helps you write a mission statement that increases your company's chance of success."

TED NICHOLAS, Author
How to Form You Own Corporation for Under $75 and
Magic Words That Bring You Riches
Indian Rocks Beach, FL

• • •

"I would describe (this) book as...raw leadership characteristics that are so fundamentally sound you will wonder why you didn't put it into this perspective yourself. I further think that the lessons to be learned from your transcript may be wasted on the "wannabe" leaders, but will more quickly make and shape those that are destined to lead."

STEVE KLEIN, Exec. VP
Epson Portland Inc., Hillsboro, OR

• • •

"This is a powerful, punchy, practical book full of great ideas you can use immediately to clarify your vision, focus your efforts and reenergize yourself in your business and your personal life! It is easy to read, easy to apply and immediately helpful in virtually everything you do."

BRIAN TRACY, President
Brian Tracy International,
Solana Beach, CA

• • •

"...not a casual read...real serious business that hit's you early and hits you hard...read it, then get to work!"

T. SCOTT GROSS, Author
Outrageous: Guilt-free Selling, Unforgettable Service
Center Point, TX

• • •

"As both a business owner and motivational speaker specializing in creating relationships for life, I found Re-Ignite Your Business! *to be a gold mine of provocative ideas which will help me move my business to a new level. This is not just another book of rehashed ideas. It's a concise, practical roadmap for getting yourself and your company on the right track to be the best you can be!"*

TONY ALESSANDRA, Ph.D., Co-Author
The Platinum Rule
La Jolla, CA
Mission: "Creating Relationships for Life"

• • •

"Our company's been very successful for 35 years, but since we've let our mission lead, we've totally transformed the taste of our food, the atmosphere in our restaurants, and our relationship with our guests. Same store sales are up 30 - 50%, and we've developed exciting, profitable new concepts. If you own a company, don't hesitate...absorb this book."

TOM MEARS, President
The Holland Inc. (BurgerVilleUSA), Vancouver, WA
Mission: "An Invitation To Trust"

• • •

"Dick Barnett has written this effective kick-in-the-pants guide in exactly the style most busy people need and appreciate: It's short, quick and to-the-point. You don't have to sift through a heap of chaff to find those kernels of truth that you can put right to work. Dick's secrets of leadership will shake you up and turn your thinking upside-down."

GEORGE WALTHER, Author
Upside-Down Marketing, Phone Power, and Power Talking
Renton, WA

• • •

Re-Ignite™

YOUR
Business!

DICK BARNETT
SHARES

THE**SECRET**OF
LEADING
WITH**CONFIDENCE,**
EASEAND**CERTAINTY**

Re-Ignite Your Business!
The Secret of Leading with Confidence, Ease and Certainty

Dick Barnett
CONFIDENT LEADER PRESS
Beaverton, Oregon

CONFIDENT LEADER PRESS
15455 NW Greenbrier Parkway, Suite 210
Beaverton, OR 97006-5700
(503) 629-5210

Confident Leader Press books may be purchased for
educational, business, or sales promotional use. Please write
or call for details.

Printed in the United States of America
First Printing: June 1997
10 9 8 7 6 5 4 3 2 1

Library of Congress Catalog Number 97-91544

Barnett, William R.
Re-Ignite Your Business! The secret of leading with confidence, ease and certainty / Dick Barnett

p. cm.

ISBN 1-890331-00-7

1. Business 2. Leadership 3. Entrepreneur
4. Self Help 5. Organizational Effectiveness
I. Title.

Cover Design and Page Layout by
Ad Graphics, Tulsa, OK
800 368-6196

Acknowledgments

This book exists because our clients let me learn from their experience with these concepts. I look forward to their comments, and I hope they discover new meaning and satisfaction from this book.

The insights of five key people underlie this book. At least three of them are unaware of the influence they've had on my work.

Robert Terry has profoundly shaped the way I view the world. The models he developed for understanding organizations (the mission/power/structure/resource diamond and matrix and the ethics ladder) are the heart of this book. I'm deeply grateful for his years of generous coaching, mentoring and sharing. Discover his latest thinking for yourself in his book "Authentic Leadership." You can reach him directly at The Terry Group, 871 Lenox Ave., St. Paul, MN 55119, telephone (612) 730-6256.

Janet Hagberg's context for understanding power is unique and key for any organization in the future. I discuss it briefly in Chapter 13. I urge you to get the full impact in her book "Real Power: Stages of Personal Power in Organizations." You can reach her directly at 7 South Sheridan, Minneapolis, MN 55405, telephone (612) 377-6629.

The model in Chapter 11 has evolved from thinking generated by Frank Burns and Linda

Nelson for the Army years ago. The best source of their version is found in "Transforming Work," edited by John Adams.

I discovered Marvin Weisbord's model about embracing confusion (Chapter 8) in a newsletter article. I can't tell you how many times it's helped leaders grasp why they find it so difficult to take an organization to a new level of performance.

Virtually every discovery I've made as a consultant has been the result of co-creation with my business partner of 12 years, Bill Kutz. His sensitivity, insights, creativity and commitment have kept our company at the cutting edge of this work. This book would never exist if he had not carried the load for our business so I could get it done.

While it's not widely recognized yet, every leader needs a coach. Bill and I were lucky when Carolyn and Jill Taylor, of The Taylor Group, based in Portland, Oregon, agreed to be ours. Their stand that we express ourselves fully and powerfully, that we serve our clients with compassionate rigor, and that we never let ourselves off the hook is largely responsible for us being of any value in the world. We wouldn't be here without their unconditional support.

Finally, my wife, Takeko, has put up with my learning curve as a Naval officer, consultant, speaker, husband and father for 30 years. Her mission is to care for those who can't care for themselves. While that's usually reflected in children and grandchildren, she's obviously applied it to me all these years as well. I'm thankful and in awe of her dedication and love.

Table of Contents

Chapter 10

Catch Your Breath! 67

A break in the action to give you time to digest what you've discovered so far, and prepare yourself to "fit on" the models and concepts in the rest of the book.

Chapter 11

Why Companies Get Off Track 69

Demonstrates why solid, action planning, goal setting, problem solving, team building organizations don't remain that way – and how you can break through the barriers.

Chapter 12

A Tool Guaranteed to Keep You On Track 75

Introduces an invaluable model that shows how to let your company's mission lead. Any problem or situation can be powerfully addressed, and effective action can be taken that is aligned with the mission.

Chapter 13

The Shocking Reality of Power 83

Most leader's understanding of power is severely limited. This model literally doubles our awareness, and shows leaders how to be genuinely empowering.

Chapter 14

More Tools for Letting the Mission Lead 93

Three startling, counter-intuitive insights essential to mission led companies: solving problems kills innovation, completing goals is often not worth the effort, and what has replaced old guarantees.

Introduction

CEOs Haven't a Clue!

Ninety-five out of 100 CEOs have no idea why their company exists! They haven't a clue. Now if you're a CEO, you're probably upset by that statement. On the other hand, if you *work* for a CEO, you're probably cheering. Whatever you do, don't dismiss the statement as outrageous. That would be a mistake.

Discover and apply the secret buried in that brash comment, and you'll elevate your organization and your leadership to exceptional new levels of performance. This book will show you how.

All leaders genuinely want to lead well. More often than not, they muddle through at best. This is not a book about fixing bad leaders. It's about helping leaders discover what's missing in their organizations, then create what's needed so they can achieve or exceed the success they're striving for.

Your people know something's missing. They'd figure it out and compensate for it if they could. But it's so subtle, few people can put their finger on it, much less generate the courage to address it.

This book suggests a unique leadership context. I urge you to absorb and apply these insights. Why? Are you working too hard? Struggling to get or maintain momentum? Losing sleep over competition? Being blind-sided by personnel issues you never expected? Don't have enough resources to do the job right? Can't quite organize things so they take care of themselves? In short, are you often frustrated by the results you're able to attain?

At a minimum, I bet you wish you were better able to transfer your experience, expertise and unique edge to your employees. Then in quiet moments by yourself, or even in the midst of a chaotic major decision, you probably wonder if you're really up to the task, if you're as good as everyone around you seems to think you are. On dark nights alone, you may wonder if you have what it takes to lead, to pull it off.

You're not alone. Most leaders have those feelings, but never admit them, even to themselves. Just recognizing your vulnerability is progress.

In fact, regardless of the amount of success you enjoy, every leader and every company can elevate their performance to a new level. Anyone can lead more powerfully and confidently, with much greater ease and certainty.

That's what this book is about. It not only gets to the heart of what's missing, it gives you the basic context, tools and technology to ensure what's missing is discovered, celebrated and used in your company in a way that will make your job easier, more enjoyable and more fulfilling.

This book offers a fresh approach, a new way to understand how and why your organization works, and how to lead it effectively. This book is the result of my life experiences, particularly of the work I've done as a leader and consultant over the past 25 years.

It's not fancy, lengthy or scholarly. I rarely read long, scholarly books myself, and I'm assuming you don't have time, either.

I promise you: it will change the way you understand organizations, lead people and do business. It can re-ignite your business.

In fact, I guarantee it. Read this book – several times if necessary. Apply these insights for yourself, with your people, in your company. Then, if you don't believe your company's performance has dramatically improved, I'll personally refund the price of this book! (You'll find a form for requesting a refund at the end of the book.)

Now turn the page and get started.

CHAPTER 1

The Source of Success

Let's begin by asking a question that will reveal a success story you already know.

Do you like pizza? Most people do.

So here's a tougher question. Do you like Domino's Pizza? Most people don't.

Well, if almost everyone likes pizza, but almost no one likes Domino's pizza, how did Domino's become the second largest pizza company in the country?

There's a secret here. If you discover that secret, and apply it to your company, you can enjoy the kind of success Domino's has experienced.

The secret is Domino's mission. What is the mission of Domino's pizza?

"Delivery!" Domino's delivers! "A pizza in 30 minutes." Period.

A pizza in 30 minutes is the reason Domino's exists. It's the reason Domino's *is*. Its reason to be.

This insight is at the heart of this book. Unlike Domino's, 95% of today's CEOs have no idea why their company really exists. They don't know their company's mission. They haven't a clue.

Many leaders take affront at the statement I just made. Surely any CEO worth his or her salt would know why their company exists.

Oh, you probably have a mission statement. It may be a sentence or two long. More likely, it's closer to a paragraph long. And then there are companies that got "serious" about their mission. Their mission statements can run on for several pages!

If you happen to lack those types of mission statements, and many entrepreneurs do, you're probably righteously declaring that your mission is "to make money," or "to create wealth for stock or stakeholders."

None of that is what I'm talking about. Lengthy mission statements are lists of platitudes. The longer they get, the more we're sure we've included everyone's pet project or special interest.

Dollar based mission statements are nonsense. Don't get me wrong, a well run business will make money. But when was the last time someone walked in your company and said, "Look, I know your mission is to make money. Since I happened to have some in my pocket, I thought I'd just drop in and leave it with you." It never happens.

No, the mission I'm talking about – *and this is critical* – is the singular, sole, solitary, core, bone-deep reason your company exists. Its reason to be.

That kind of mission can – and must – be expressed in just a few words. Five or fewer is ideal. Like – "A pizza in 30 minutes."

That's why Domino's exists. They don't claim to exist to provide you a good pizza! Have you ever heard them promise you a hot pizza? Heck, they don't even promise you the pizza you ordered!

Domino's simply says, call us – then trust us. We'll put something together, heat it up, slap in a box, and hand it to a 16 year-old daredevil driver who will deliver it to your door – all in 30 minutes or less!

Now *that's* a mission – a reason to be!

It works – and Domino's is very successful – for two reasons: everyone knows exactly what it is, and it's easy for anyone to remember. Including you – who never eats their product.

And what about your company? What is the sole, singular, solitary, core, bone-deep reason your company exists? Can you answer that question in five words or less? If not, it's missing for you and your people.

So what? Why is that important?

Very simply, if your core mission is missing, I guarantee it's slowing your progress and hindering your success. And it's contributing to the chaos that makes your job as a leader more difficult than necessary.

Keep reading. We're about to take a closer look at this concept of mission, and your company's mission, in the next chapter.

CHAPTER 2

The Heart of the Matter

The diamond model illustrated below can change your life! Understand and apply it, and I guarantee it will change your organization. It will take you to new levels of productivity and performance.

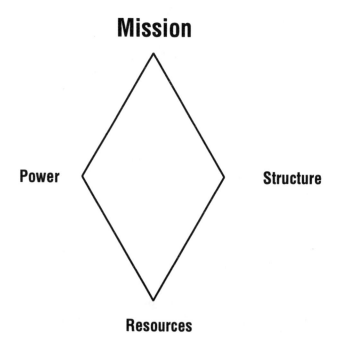

Mission

Power

Structure

Resources

This is just the first of several models throughout this book that evolved from the creative genius of Robert W. Terry. Before we get into it, I want to introduce you to the man behind the ideas.

Working in the Detroit ghettos in the 1960's, Bob Terry created a triangle model that allowed blacks and whites to discover shared meaning in the face of active violence.[1] His context literally saved my neck when I was dealing with race-based unrest as a Naval officer in the 1970's.

As Bob applied his thinking to businesses and other organizations, he expanded the triangle into this diamond, which served as the basis of his teaching and consulting for many years. He generously shared his thinking with me again in the early 1980's when I was responsible for developing the curriculum for training organizational development specialists in the Navy.

Then later, in the 1980's, Bill Kutz and I were developing our consulting practice, while Bob founded and directed the Reflective Leadership Center, Hubert H. Humphrey Institute of Public Affairs, University of Minnesota. The three of us frequently shared discoveries and insights as Bill and I used Bob's notions as the foundation of our work with leaders of organizations committed to breaking through existing barriers or plateaus.

More recently, as head of The Terry Group, he's rounded the diamond into an interlocking, dual layered wheel for leadership action. While he's published that concept,[2] the diamond has never received widespread attention. Its simplicity and power is one of the reasons I've written this book.

---

[1] Terry, Robert W. *For Whites Only*. Grand Rapids: Eerdmans, 1970

[2] Terry, Robert W. *Authentic Leadership: Courage in Action*. San Francisco: Jossey-Bass, 1993

Bob's generosity and gracious support has been critical to my development and success. You will find his influence throughout this book. Any misinterpretations or misapplications are strictly mine. Once you've applied the concepts we're discussing here, you'll find Bob's other works extremely valuable to your development as a confident leader.

Now let's get into the model. We'll look at each point of the diamond in some detail as we go on, but I want to begin with "mission."

As we said in the last chapter, your company's mission is the core reason your company exists. It's the reason your company is in business. Why your company *is*. The very reason for your company to *be*.

I'm going to stay with this a minute because more often than not, leaders get this confused.

Mission is *not* your vision for the future of your company.

Mission is *not* your goals or objectives.

Mission is *not* something you're going toward, or even something you're trying to become.

Mission is what your company *is*. Why your company *exists*.

Your mission existed in full bloom the day you first opened your doors. It exists today, in full bloom, in the midst of the mire that is getting in your way, hindering your success. And it will exist tomorrow or next year as the anchor, the bedrock, the core reason your company *is*.

Let's go back to Domino's. Domino's exists to deliver each and every pizza in 30 minutes. That was true the day it began, it's true today, and it will be true tomorrow.

Often companies confuse who they are with what they do. Domino's is even more at risk about that than most companies, since its reason to exist could be perceived as what they do.

When they first opened their doors, Domino's might have been forgiven if they had said something like, "I know we're in the business of a pizza in 30 minutes, but we're new at this, and don't have all the systems in place yet. Let's see if we can get this first pizza there in a couple of hours!"

They didn't say that. That first pizza was delivered in 30 minutes, just like every other pizza since, or, in those early days, they gave it to the customer for free.

I don't know how many free pizzas Domino's had to deliver before they got the time within 30 minutes, but they never changed, or denied, their mission, their reason to exist: a pizza in 30 minutes. That tenacity to their purpose, that commitment is what created the second largest pizza company in the country.

Here are two more keys to a successful mission, that Domino's clearly illustrates.

First: the mission must be easy to remember – by everyone. It can't be long and involved. It can't be convoluted. It must be crystal clear to anyone who comes in contact with it. After all, *you* knew what Domino's mission was, and you may never have eaten a Domino's pizza!

Second: everyone – inside or out of your company – should know your mission cold! Every cook, delivery driver and order taker knows Domino's mission. They don't just know it, they *live* it. And here's the shocker. *You know and live it, too!* Don't believe me? Think about this.

You've driving down a narrow city street, with cars parked on both sides. You look up and see a beat up old VW with the lighted Domino's bucket hanging from the bent-over antenna coming straight at you. What do you do? Of course, you pull over to make sure they have room. Any sane person would.

Now, same scenario, except this time you look up and there's a Pizza Hut truck coming at you. What do you do? Keep going. You assume they'll drive safely, don't you?

This vignette dramatizes two key features of any good mission. One, it's very easy to remember, and two, everyone knows it. In Domino's case, everyone, including you, does everything they can to help the driver on Domino's mission succeed! Including getting out of their way!

What would your company be like if everyone was committed to the reason it existed, and was totally aligned with its success? That's the focus of this book, and mission is at the heart of the matter. Keep reading.

CHAPTER 3

Real Missions

By now, perhaps, you're a little tired of hearing about Domino's Pizza. It's easy to suspect Domino's is unique. What works there won't work in other companies.

The fact is, clear, core missions *do* change companies. Here are three real examples. First, a hospital.

Most hospitals today probably feel they have dealt with the mission question. If you boil down the typical, rather lengthy hospital mission statement, it usually reduces to something like: "Quality Care, Quality Service, Affordable Cost."

Even expressed that simply, hospital missions still are three-headed monsters. One year the focus is on improving the quality of care by hiring more technically skilled doctors. The next budget cycle the new wing, computerized patient records, even high-tech bedpans get the lion's share of the resources. The third year focuses on belt tightening because costs have gotten out of line. In fact, even though it's only six words long, that typical hospital mission is like trying to stand together as a group on a waterbed! You can't do it with any ease, grace or alignment.

One hospital in a large HMO broke through these issues when it simply defined its mission as "Healthy Members."

The obvious skeptical question is, "Great, but how is the patient who will die in the next half hour a healthy member?" Staff in this hospital had a simple answer. "Our job is to see that he or she is as healthy as possible for their last half hour."

To everyone's surprise, the mission worked. The normal debates about treatment protocols, cures vs. containment, surgical decisions, equipment purchases and usage and the role of wellness or prevention all changed. Everyone from night nurses to interns, assistant administrators to neurosurgeons, receptionists answering telephones to janitors polishing floors felt they could directly contribute to Healthy Members. Even the atmosphere of the place was different. HMO members were heard to proudly call it "my hospital!"

When the national accreditation committee made its formal inspection they were actually mystified. "Why is this place so different?" they puzzled. "It's not like any other hospital." The staff openly attributed that difference to the mission. But a mission driven hospital is such a rarity, the inspectors never quite accepted that response. In the end it didn't matter, because the hospital passed the accreditation inspection with flying colors.

For a second example, let's go high-tech. A manufacturing division of a Fortune 500 company was dying. A couple of years earlier the Koreans had begun making a product very similar to this division's flagship – for one-tenth the cost.

Nothing the company did – layoffs, cost cutting, reorganizing, training programs – made any measurable impact. Both division and corporate leaders were at their wit's end.

Key leaders finally re-examined why the division existed at all, and had to make up a word that defined their mission: "Manufuturing."

That's no typo. The team realized if they had any future at all, it was in their own hands – and they had to make it up as they went along. Corporate couldn't help. The Koreans weren't going away. They literally had to reinvent themselves from scratch.

We'll return to this company later, but for now suffice it to say that *by letting "manufuturing" lead them for the next 18 months this manufacturing division not only got out of red ink, they developed seven totally new products, three of which actually got successfully to market!* Clarity of purpose, of why you exist, does work – even when it's totally made up.

Finally, how about a trucking company? Since deregulation, trucking has been a cutthroat industry. To get the business, truckers lie through their teeth. They know if they don't get the shipment loaded on their trucks, their competition (which can't deliver either) will get the business.

A typical exchange might sound like this:

Seattle Shipper: "I need this in San Diego by 8:00 tomorrow morning, I don't want to pay for special service, and it's now 5:00 p.m. Can you get it there?"

Trucking dispatcher: "Sure we can." (Of course he's lying. It's physically impossible by truck.) "We're here to serve. Thanks for not calling our competition!"

Seattle shipper, noon the next day, when the truck with the shipment is still north of San Francisco, and the San Diego customer is irate: "Where is it? You promised it would be there by 8:00 a.m. If you bill me for this foul-up, I'll never do business with you again."

Truck dispatcher: "Well, it was a calculated risk," (still lying) "but we'll hustle it on down there tonight, and of course we won't charge you for the delivery."

While this may sound farfetched, it's how many truckers slowly went broke. One trucking company took itself out of this self-defeating contest, and declared its mission to be, "We Keep Our *Customer's* Promises."

Read that again. It's subtle. The trucker *stopped* saying they would keep impossible promises to shippers. They now said they would keep promises *shippers* made to *their* customers! This was an entirely different ball game.

Now when the Seattle shipper calls at 5:00 p.m. the conversation is different.

Truck dispatcher: "What's the promise you made to your San Diego customer?"

Seattle shipper: "That I'd have it to them by 8:00 tomorrow morning."

Truck dispatcher: "Are you going to keep that promise?"

Seattle shipper: "Of course, that's why I called you."

Truck dispatcher: "Good. I'll pick it up in an hour, drive it to the airport, put it on a commercial flight if possible, or otherwise charter a plane. Either way, I guarantee it will be delivered to your customer in San Diego at 8:00 a.m. as you promised. I'll send you an invoice as soon as I know the cost."

Seattle shipper, sputtering: "Are you kidding? That will cost a fortune! I'll call your competition."

Truck dispatcher: "Do you really believe our competition will get it there by 8:00 a.m.?"

Seattle shipper: "No, but one of you wants the business bad enough to wind up delivering it for me free because you didn't perform."

Truck dispatcher: "So you're saying you're *not* going to keep your promise to San Diego. Is that right?"

Obviously the conversation can take several turns from here, but you get the idea. As a result of this transforming mission, this trucking company had an opportunity not only to create entirely new relationships with its shippers, it discovered many profitable possibilities from the "keeping the promises you make to your customers" mission that had never been considered a part of trucking before.

These three real-life examples demonstrate that clarity of mission is not limited to delivering pizzas fast.

Before we dig into mission further, the next chapter will examine the second corner of the diamond model, power. I bet power's not what you think it is.

CHAPTER 4

Get Comfortable with Power

In America we have a love-hate relationship with power. Most of us want more power. But if we admit it publicly, we risk being called power-hungry. When someone else acts powerfully, we accuse them of being on a power trip.

As a result, power is rarely discussed openly in corporations. Instead, most meaningful conversations about power only occur as gossip in cliques.

Not dealing freely with power isn't just unhealthy, it's deadly.

The power we fear, suppress or repress isn't real power; so let's redefine it. *Power, in this fresh context, is the actual expenditure of energy.* Everyone expends energy. Therefore, everyone is always powerful. The danger, and damage, occurs when we *don't* talk openly about how that energy is being spent.

Don't believe me? What if I said some of the most powerful people in your organization are your *worst* performers! These are the folks that spend most of their energy *avoiding* being productive. As a result, you spend much of your energy just trying to keep tabs on what they're actually doing.

Now I'm realistic; there will always be a bottom 10%. The problem arises because we don't talk about the dynamics of power directly, openly, and often.

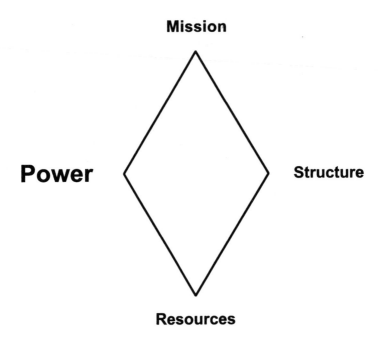

Mission

Power

Structure

Resources

Everyone spends their energy at work. Effective people spend their energy creating, achieving, producing, accomplishing, innovating, coaching, leading. They're powerful.

But other people are just as effective. They may even have *more* effect because they spend their energy delaying, reneging, sabotaging, hiding, resisting, destroying, withholding. They, too, are powerful.

So everyone is powerful. Since power is the actual expenditure of energy, everyone expends their energy one way or the other.

The secret for organizations is to talk about power – what people are actually *doing* – all the time. Why? Because effective organizations know they will fulfill their mission – be who they say they are – more thoroughly when everyone's energy is focused on *being* the mission.

At Domino's everyone spends their energy getting that next pizza there within 30 minutes. "Healthy Members" and "We Keep Our Customer's Promises" altered the way energy is invested in a hospital and a trucking company. "Manufuturing" actually *generates* energy in everyone involved. In that case, there is no future if they aren't all fully invested and contributing.

So let's pause a minute to recognize *a critical insight.* Remember that most organizations have no clear mission; no core reason to exist. And power is a taboo subject, not often discussed in organizations.

When those two key elements are missing, *companies struggle and suffer unnecessarily.* And they *are* missing in 95% of all companies in America today.

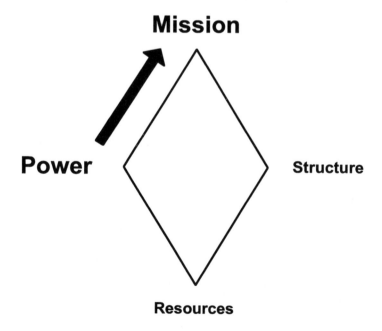

In contrast, when the core mission *is* clear to everyone, power conversations actually *generate* results.

Everyone spends their energy on some mission. When your company's mission is clear, most of that energy can be focused on fulfilling its mission. Isn't that what you want?

But, if your corporate mission is *not* clear, people are spending their energy on their *own* missions, which usually have nothing to do with your company or even their job. That's the state of most organizations today.

Your people *want* to work. They want to contribute their energy, enthusiasm and expertise. But if there's no meaningful, fulfilling mission to attract their contribution and energy, they'll find something else more compelling to align their energy with, and just go through the motions at work.

This is the best argument I know for clarifying and broadcasting your company's mission. As long as it's not clear and in place, you're losing a huge percentage of your people's energy – and paying them for it anyway.

Here's one more thing to think about. It makes perfect sense that most organizations don't talk openly about power. In fact, it would be disastrous if we did!

Why? Because people are spending their energy on *some* mission. Since there's no clear corporate mission, you probably don't *want* to know how your people are *really* spending their energy while they're at work.

If you did know, you'd be even harder pressed to lead them. Why? Because the mission they're actually fulfilling, even if they aren't clear what it is, is a lot more powerful than your personal powers of persuasion. Think about it. That's probably why you often feel you're working harder than you want to, or than ought to be necessary.

But let's move on. What happens in a mission-led company? Turn to the next chapter and we'll explore an example.

CHAPTER 5

A Real Mission in Action

The easiest way to describe an organization led by a mission is to focus on actions in a single, mission-led company. Remember the high-tech "manufuturing" division? Here are three situations that highlight innovation, discipline and productivity in this mission led organization.

Innovation. If ever there were a time for doubts about turning leadership over to a mission, it's when the mission is a freshly created, figment of the groups' imagination! Yet within minutes of declaring this manufuturing mission, the process began. One member of the group turned to another and asked, "Do you still have an idea for a new product you want us to develop?"

"Absolutely," the other person shot back. "Each year I request $200,000 in my budget so I can build a prototype. It's always the first item to get cut."

"If you can put your hands on $20,000, I know how we can create a prototype," the questioner stated, matter-of-factly. And that was the beginning. Within 18 months, as I reported in Chapter 3, this manufacturing division developed seven new products.

Think about this for a minute. Before there was a core mission, both people in this scenario were aware of this idea, but were powerless to do anything about it. But once the mission was defined, the process instantly became effortless.

What's the secret here? First, not much happens until you're clear about the reason for it to exist. And second, no one is empowered to break out of the preexisting constraints until the mission creates the space for them to step into.

There's an added secret in this story that reveals why empowerment doesn't work in most organizations. Can you see it? We'll come back to it in Chapter 14.

In the meantime, let's continue our exploration of what life was like when led by the mission of manufuturing.

Discipline. Discipline is different in a mission driven organization. When someone's action caught the division head's attention, she would stop, turn to the individual and say, "I'm confused. How is what you're doing manufuturing?"

She always got one of two answers. Usually the person excitedly described how what they were doing was manufuturing to them. The division head then had several options. She either congratulated them and moved on, got very excited and called an "instant meeting" so others could see "manufuturing" in action, or simply said, "I don't get it as clearly as you do yet," and moved on without more comment.

The second type of response she got usually began with a blank stare and a muttered, "Gee, Boss, I don't know." In this case, the division head was always decisive: "Then do something that is!"

And she would immediately refocus her attention on something else.

Is this really discipline? You bet. In fact, it was all she could do. After all, she didn't know what was, or was not, manufuturing any more than anyone else. She was totally dependent on people generating value from within that mission. If they did, she recognized it. If they didn't, she couldn't do a whole lot about it – but she never condoned wasted energy.

Although this situation may sound pretty loose, the outcome of these interactions was amazing. People felt acknowledged and challenged by the first response, or became very reflective as a result of the second.

In fact, no person was ever able to admit more than three times that they couldn't align their work with manufuturing! If they couldn't, it became evident to those individuals that they were not connected or compelled by this mission, and they realized they didn't belong in this company any longer. They quit – gratefully!

Virtually every person leaving the company, (and about 10% did) made a comment like, "Thank God we clarified this mission. It's perfect for this group and this company, but it's not what I want to do with my life. I'm so glad I discovered that now, rather than hang around for the next 5 years wondering why I wasn't effective or happy!"

Productivity. An ordinary staff meeting about eight months after the mission was declared demonstrated the power of manufuturing on productivity. One of the agenda items for the meeting was a demand from corporate that this division give back $200,000 from its budget that quarter – and it was already the second week of the third month.

To start the process, the division head turned to the first of about eight direct-reports and asked, "How much can you give us, Tom?" When Tom finished, he had offered up about $180,000 from his department alone! "Gee, Tom," someone quipped, "we needed $200,000, and that's only 180 grand."

"Well," Tom replied, "there's over $20,000 on the back of this sheet. I didn't read it off because it's just small change."

When they completed the circuit of the table, this group, which had been more than $15,000,000 in the red just a few months earlier, had offered more than $2,500,000 back to corporate!

I thought they were pulling my leg, and said so. They got mad. "Do you know something we don't know?" they asked. "Isn't this a serious request from corporate?"

After assuring them I was skeptical, not deceitful, I asked them how they thought they could really give this much back? "Easy," one replied. "We manufuture. We'll manufuture with whatever resources we have. If corporate needs this money, let them have it."

There's another secret about letting the mission lead that's revealed by this profound statement: *When you're clear about your mission, you have all the resources you'll ever need!* The resources – people, inventory, ideas, raw materials, or in this case, dollars – just show up. I'm not asking you to believe me, but I am saying if you test it, you'll find it true.

I can't end this chapter without reporting corporate's response to the division's 2.5 million dollar offer: "No, thanks, that's okay. Just give us $200,000. After all, every division has to give their fair share." It makes you wonder.

But in reality, corporate's response is normal. When companies don't know why they exist, they focus on the other two corners of the diamond: structure and resources. Now you're ready to look at those in an entirely fresh way.

CHAPTER 6

The Siren Song of Structure and Resources

So if 95% of all companies don't have a core mission, and it's taboo in most companies to talk about power, what happens? We spend an enormous amount of energy on the other two corners of the diamond: structure and resources.

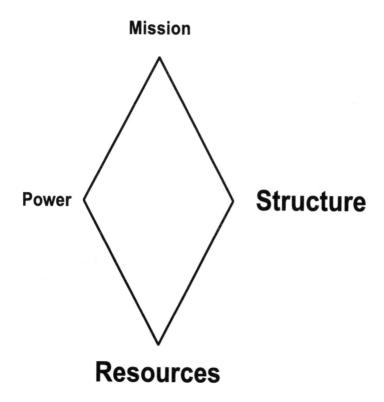

Mission

Power

Structure

Resources

Obviously, structures and resources are essential in any organization. But they aren't the reason the company exists, nor are they what pulls forth energy.

Structures are supports. They support people so they can spend their power being the mission. Common structures are the company's goals, objectives, action plans, organization charts, processes and mechanism. Structures are conduits that enable the mission to be fulfilled, the framework that supports the energy being expended on the mission.

Resources are anything which can be used to fulfill the mission. People, money, inventory, bricks, mortar and machinery obviously are resources, but less tangible things such as ideas, experience, skills and talents are, too. In fact, from this perspective, even problems, issues, concerns and breakdowns are resources as well. They are all things which can be channeled through supportive structures to generate energy to be the mission.

Remember the old cliché: "We don't have problems, we have opportunities"? If you're like most leaders, you nodded and smiled at this, but you really didn't buy it. Just more "consultant babble."

Well, from this perspective, it can be true. When you're clear about the mission, *anything* may turn out to be a valuable resource. In fact, as we saw in manufuturing, the bigger the breakdown, the bigger the possibility of breakthrough.

But most leaders don't want breakdowns, and devote most of their energy toward avoiding them. Take a look at what happens in companies every day.

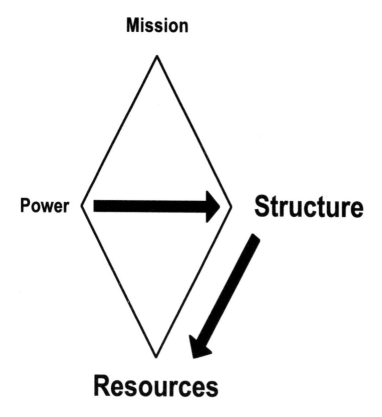

Notice how, if we don't have a mission and we can't talk openly about power, we go to structure and resources with a vengeance!

Have you ever been in this situation? Sure you have, and if you're like most good leaders, you decide to get organized. You pack up the key folks and head for the mountains or the beach for a goal setting, action planning, problem solving, strategic thinking, team building retreat.

You've got good people who care. The retreat is a success. Solid, achievable goals are generated and agreed to; strategic and actions plans are developed and sworn to in blood; problems which have been brewing for months are resolved and there's a palpable sense of teamwork and camaraderie within the group. Most importantly, everyone commits to "really doing it" this time.

You head back to the office, and everything goes great – for a while. But then deadlines start to slip. Costs exceed expectations. New schisms develop within the team. You become frustrated and resigned. Will it ever get any better really?

At about that moment, one of your stars, who's missed two of their three key deadlines, knocks at your door. "Got a minute, Boss?"

"Of course," you sigh, "but before you begin, what's happening with that goal you agreed to?"

"I'm glad you asked," he replies. "I'm still excited about it, but we've run into some unexpected hurdles. I'll only need another $100,000 and two more full time people from Design, and we'll be sailing smoothly. If you'll call finance and authorize it, I'll go to work on the designers."

You blow. "I tell you what. I'll give you the next three minutes of my time to handle what you came in for. Period. Then you get back down to your office and deliver with the people and dollars you've got. That *is* what you committed to do at the beach!"

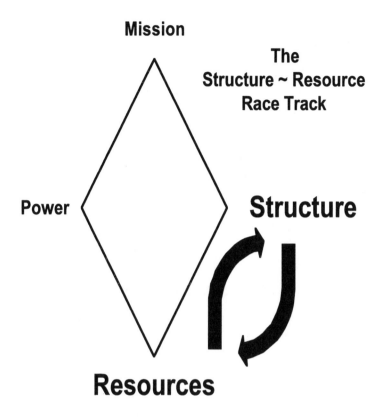

Mission

The Structure ~ Resource Race Track

Power   **Structure**

Resources

Look what happened here. Once we're caught on the racetrack between structures and resources, there's no way out. Every conversation becomes a manipulation to alter the structures and gain access to resources.

This dynamic is precisely the source of belief systems which assume there's "only so much (fill in the blank with your scarcest resource) to go around, and I have to fight for my share." In a very real sense, everyone on this racetrack is powerless. Sure, some will win more often than others.

But ultimately, nothing succeeds to its full potential, particularly your company. It doesn't have to be this way.

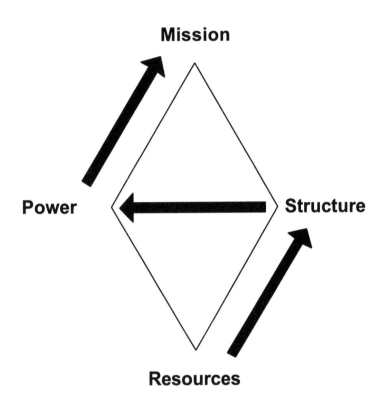

Let's review. There's nothing inherently wrong with resources and structures. In fact, they are essential to any organization. But most leaders misunderstand their importance. And they misunderstand it because they don't have a mission, and they don't talk about power.

When it works, it works like this. Resources must be channeled through conduits (structures) that support people's energy (power) so they can spend it fulfilling the mission.

This is the core secret to any organization's success. Leaders who don't grasp and apply this secret may still succeed. But they're going to work much harder, and probably suffer much more, than is necessary while they do.

You can be a leader who succeeds with ease and certainty! Begin right now by discovering the core reason your company exists, its mission. We'll talk about how to do that in the next chapter.

CHAPTER 7

Find Your Company's Mission

G et this truth clear right from the start: *you won't "think" your way to your company's mission.* It comes from the gut, not the head. No wonder rational, clearheaded business people rarely discover the mission!

Think about all the long-winded, platitude-laden, politically-correct, socially-conscious mission statements you routinely encounter. All of these came from the head. They were written because they sounded good, suggested an image, included everyone's pet agenda, or, as participants often admit later, "just to get all the data on newsprint sheets hung around the room into some order so we can get on with our *real* reason for being here – to get something done!"

Core mission comes from the soul, and it takes some soul searching to discover it.

Question: Who should declare a company's mission? Answer: Those who have the authentic right and responsibility to do so. If you're a sole proprietor or owner, it's probably up to you alone. Otherwise, you'll probably be more successful if it's a group (they're not yet a team) effort.

Let's deal with the individual owner first. What gets you out of bed in the morning? That's a great place to start looking for the reason you created or bought your company. There's something that drives you at that level that's important.

When they start this exploration, most people initially offer competitive or survival answers: "Make money." "Be the best." "Kill the competition." "Feed the family." Those are all fine, but they're not the mission. Look deeper.

The next level usually is altruistic or noble answers: "I want to serve others." "We're the quality producer." "I want to make a difference." These "motherhood and apple pie" responses aren't it either. Keep going deeper.

It gets tougher from here on. To help you get to it, ask yourself what's important about the answers you expressed above. What's important about serving others? What's important about quality? What's important about making a difference?

Keep asking that question, getting more answers: What's important about that? Then ask, what's important about that? Keep going. What's important about that? Keep asking until something goes "thunk" in your heart. It probably will take your breath away. *Now* you're getting close to the *real* reason your company exists.

No one can predict the mission. They certainly can't give one to you. It can only come from your heart, and it's unique to you and your company.

That factor is what makes mission-led companies so powerful and successful; they're unique, and they know it. No other company exists for exactly the same reason, even when it seems so obvious that *everyone* must exist for that reason.

Surely every hospital must exist for "healthy members," right? Well they don't. And no other company would dream of existing to "manufuture." Those missions went "thunk" when they were discovered. That distinction is what you're seeking for your company in this process.

Here's another reality you need to be aware of: you may be shocked or embarrassed by some of the insights you uncover. One family owned business in the midst of this process discovered their company only existed so they could get revenge on each other! They sold the business, got divorced, rarely speak to each other, but are infinitely happier than they ever were trying to make that business work.

While that level of venom is rare, it's not unusual for a leader, when asked what was important about a response they just gave, to reply with an answer like "to prove my Dad wrong!" or "because my last employer fired me." These aren't missions, but they are important clues. Don't deny or gloss over them. What *is* important about proving yourself, or being fired? Keep digging. You'll know you're there when your response goes "thunk."

Now that you know what's involved in the process, you'll be better able to hear what I'm about to say next. Most leaders, even sole proprietors, can't get to their company's mission alone. That's not because they're incapable. It's because we're so used to thinking our way through questions like this, we're reluctant to let ourselves go on an emotional roller coaster like this process. But don't let that prevent you from discovering your company's mission.

You'll have trouble getting out of your head and into your heart, so ask for help. Find someone who has no stake in the outcome to support you by asking the "what's important about that?" questions as you let yourself go into the source of mission. The result will be truer, and there's a surprising benefit. It's quite likely your helper will become the first person who totally understands why your company exists, and what you're accomplishing. That's a nice ally to have, even if they don't work for you!

Now let's take this process to a larger group or company. You probably can discover your organization's mission in a day or two. First decide who will take part. Again, who has the authentic right and responsibility to be there? While cross sections may work for a small percentage of companies, the dynamics of that grouping usually lengthen the process unnecessarily. Everyone's just too concerned about looking good in front of people with a different status in the company. Instead, get the key leaders in the room. Eight, or less, is ideal. Fifteen to twenty at the most. Then proceed as follows:

- Brainstorm and list all the **accomplishments** of the last six months to a year. Write them on newsprint and post them around the walls. You'll all be utterly amazed at the magnitude of what you've actually achieved.

- Now – and this is critical – **acknowledge** those accomplishments. Everyone must recognize, and really absorb what's been achieved. (There's a secret here: People never really move ahead until they've been acknowledged for what they've done! Apply this secret frequently, and you'll see dramatic changes in behavior throughout your organization!).

- Next, have people identify concerns, barriers, or **problems** they are currently, or soon will be, facing. List these and post them, too. You're not going to address or resolve these issues now. The point is to acknowledge their existence and reality, and ensure every person's concerns have been heard.

- You're now ready to ask each individual what they **want**. This is the heart of the process. What compels each person in this group *is* why the company exists. Just as we did with a sole proprietor, you'll need to keep asking "what's important about that?" Get to as deep a "want" as you can, and record each participant's final "want" on newsprint. You'll be amazed at the power and depth of the drives people share. This is truly a special, sacred experience.

- At some point during this part of the process, someone usually makes a comment like, "Gee, I want what each one of you people want!" Others instantly agree, and that's the key. *Genuine wants rarely conflict!* Yes, when true wants are revealed at this level, they don't conflict with each other. In fact, they'll be very easy to align with the mission.

- When each person's wants are posted, ask a powerful, simple question: "If that's what each of you want – and we agree we all want what each other wants – why is this group of people in this company, at this moment in time?"

That's a **destiny question**. Asking it will begin to reveal your company's mission. If you've gotten to each individual's genuine core "want," the mission will probably go "thunk" a couple of minutes into this dialogue. Don't be discouraged if it takes longer, but stay at the depth you've taken the discussion. You're very close to the real reason your company or organization exists.

- When you have the mission, say it in just a handful of words – the fewer the better – two, three or four preferably – six to eight at the most. That ensures you're declaring the *core* mission, not a "conglomerate" mission of several notions or ideals.

Obviously, this is only a brief summary of processes that will help you discover the single, core, bone-deep reason your company exists. And, of course, there are other ways to get to it. The point is, you must let the mission surface powerfully and emotionally, not intellectually. That may be scary. It is more than a little out of control. There likely will be tears, and some pain. All that's normal. The discovery is not just worth it, it's essential for your company. Go for it!

By the way, there's an unexpected outcome of this process. Remember, at the beginning of this chapter, I said if you did this with a group they were not yet a team? By the end of this experience that group will have become a genuine team. It's a subtle, unanticipated outcome, but the alignment that occurs when people publicly acknowledge their accomplishments and fears, and reveal their deepest desires, bonds them more powerfully and effectively than most structured, direct team-building processes. Participants will operate with an entirely new level of respect, cooperation and effectiveness in the future. Congratulations!

CHAPTER 8

Why Most Leaders Won't Get This Far

Companies that know why they exist have had a major breakthrough. Most companies never do. If you're stuck, or fear you'll never discover your mission, let's break up what's keeping you there. Marvin Weisbord credits Swedish social psychologist Claes Janssen with the model on the next page.[3] We've expanded it beyond their original intentions, but if you apply it, you *will* get unstuck.

Let's face it. We all like to be comfortable. We like to "have it handled" and "working smoothly." When something happens that makes us uncomfortable, we try and fix it as quickly as possible. That's the source of most problem solving and goal setting which passes for leadership in companies today. If those efforts don't work, more often than not we go to denial. "It'll get better as soon as the economy improves," or "We're just growing. You have to expect the unexpected, and roll with the punches. Chin up!"

---

[3] Weisbord, Marvin R. *Productive Workplaces: Organizing and Managing for Dignity, Meaning and Community,* pp. 266-70, San Francisco: Jossey-Bass. 1987.

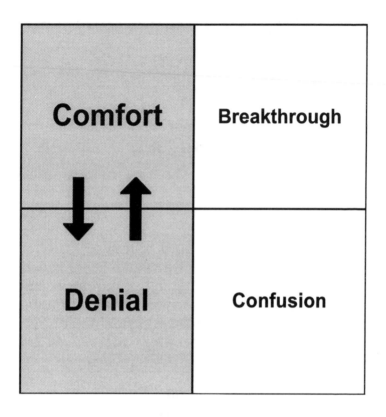

Although these statements may sound or feel encouraging, they are simply a denial of reality. It's not working! And few of us want to face that. Instead, the denial allows us to scamper back to being comfortable, for the moment, at least.

Unfortunately, many leaders vacillate their entire careers between comfort and denial. You see this dynamic in all companies, but it's prevalent in those which achieve a clear level of success quickly. "Hey, this is a great concept or product! People want it. Just keep doing what we're doing, and we can't miss! In fact, let's expand right now, ahead of schedule."

The more that works, the harder it seems to be for leaders to face reality when it stops working. A large furniture, appliance and electronics retailer fit this mold. Even when its showrooms and parking lots were empty, its CEO continued to bounce between comfort and denial. The company went bankrupt, and took at least one major supplier with it.

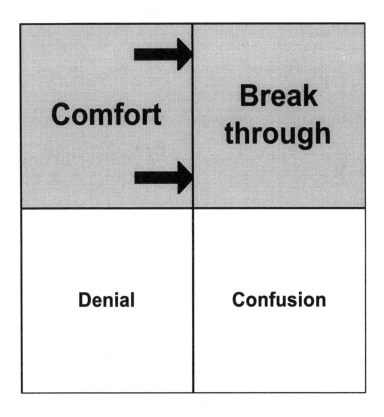

Other leaders, recognizing the futility of denial, go directly for a breakthrough. This is behind most reorganization, redesign, re-engineering efforts. We're not comfortable, so let's go directly to breakthrough.

Here's the bad news. You can't go directly to breakthrough. There's no door from "fat, dumb, and happy" to the next level of performance. And most of us will try to find it at least once. Many will waste enormous amounts of energy and resources over and over in futile attempts. This is what's happening when an instant fix, system-of-the-month, or the latest fad is embraced and implemented. It's why those fixes never work over time.

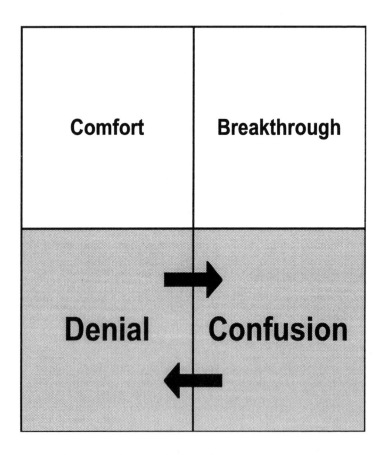

The way beyond that barrier is to recognize our denial. Once we do that, the only way out is *through* the denial. And that's very confusing.

It's not easy to tolerate profound confusion, so you'll find you return to denial often. The secret is to get very curious about the confusion. Respect it, live in it, learn from it, and you'll achieve the breakthrough you're seeking, usually when you least expect it.

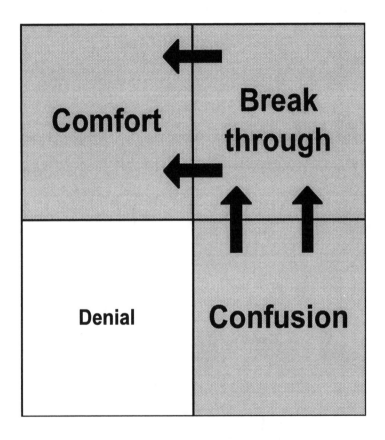

But don't get too cocky. Breakthroughs are difficult to maintain. While there's no door to get directly from comfort to breakthrough, there *is* a door, almost a chute, that leads directly from breakthrough back to comfort. As soon as we achieve the breakthrough, we're instantly relieved and comfortable again. That feels good for the moment, but it's actually counterproductive. Why? Because as soon as it occurs to you that that's what has happened, you're probably going to deny it. And the process starts all over again. In the meantime, the breakthrough is weakening or being lost altogether. The only effective action is to acknowledge your denial, embrace your new confusion, and from there, be ready for a new breakthrough.

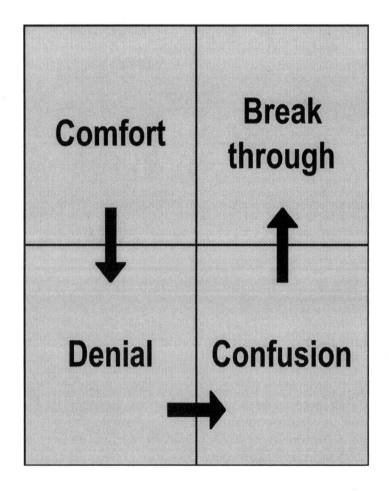

And now for the challenge. We've already seen that most leaders spend their lives vacillating between comfort and denial. Once you grasp the essential power and relationship of confusion and breakthroughs, you'll spend your life vacillating between those two, which puts a severe limit on your opportunities to just be "comfortable."

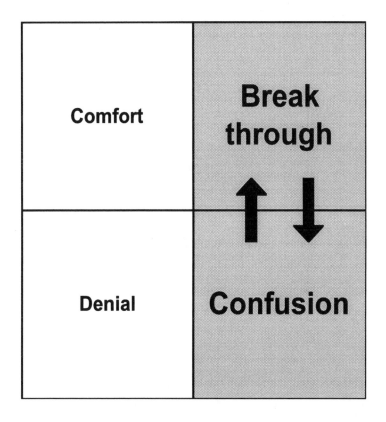

No wonder so few leaders are willing to make this commitment. But it's the choice you face, and the choice you must make, if you're going to let your mission lead you and your company – because mission-led companies usually are confusing and abound in breakthroughs (remember manufuturing).

There's one more piece of thinking that must be jolted to ensure you have the space to fulfill your company's mission. Get ready for another huge "a-ha" in the next chapter.

CHAPTER 9

Is Your Structure in the Way?

Y ou may find it hard to accept, but *nobody gets out of bed in the morning to make your best structure work!* It's critical that you understand this, or you won't be able to let your new mission lead.

Most leaders assume that organizations work like the left-hand column on the next page. Starting at the bottom, the thinking goes something like this: you people (resources) come spend your energy (power) to make our company (structure) successful (mission).

While that sounds good, there's a problem: most companies don't have a mission. Therefore, the reality is: people are invited to spend their energy to make a *structure* work. How uninspiring! Nobody comes to work to make the organization chart live!

Instead, look at the right-hand column. This describes a mission-led organization. Again, starting at the bottom, you people (resources) come use our company (structure) to support your energy (power) so we can all be who we say we are (mission).

We Invert Power and Structure

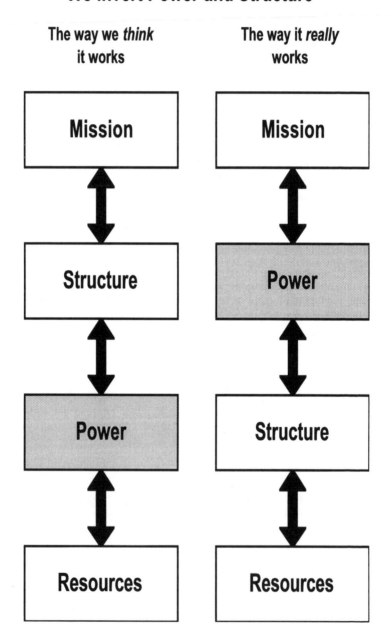

Get the difference? Most don't. Nine times out of ten leaders *invert* power and structure.

It's critical that you understand your company from the Mission, Power, Structure, Resources paradigm, not Mission, Structure, Power, Resources. Why is this important? Because when you understand and act from this relationship, there is nothing between your people's energy and the mission. There is space for the mission to really lead. It's a "straight shot" to success!

Inverting Power and Structure Hinders Success!

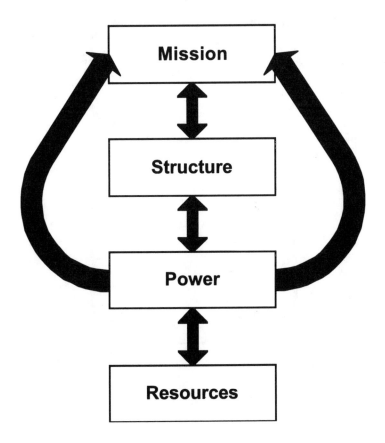

Even if a company has a clear core mission, but misunderstands this sequence, they'll still suffer and struggle much more than is necessary. As you can see, folks grasp the mission, but still spend enormous amounts of energy trying to get *around* those structures you're so proud of! I know you've worked hard to define the structure and put it in place. That doesn't stop it from being a barrier between your people and the mission! Sorry, Boss, I wish I could make it easier, but your paradigm has to shift.

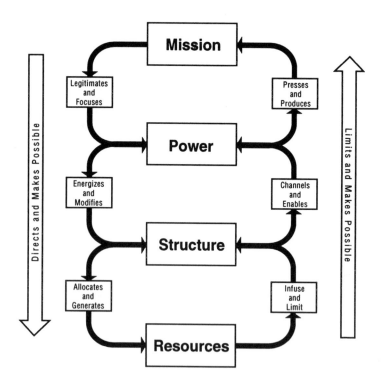

This is a key context for understanding your mission-led company. Once again, Bob Terry elegantly demonstrates the whole process in this diagram. The more you absorb it, the more clearly you'll internalize the dynamic and make it your own.

Before we leave the subject of paradigms, you need one more picture to understand the dynamics which are working in your organization every day. This is important because it demonstrates why so many well intended efforts to let the mission lead fail – not because of outside factors, but because of forces *within* the company! Read on, but first...

CHAPTER 10

Catch Your Breath!

How are you doing? You're probably pretty excited, so it's time to pause, catch your breath and digest what you've discovered already, before you begin the second half of this journey.

I originally wrote this book so you could throw it in your briefcase, climb on an airplane, fly from Dallas to Chicago, read the whole thing enroute, and be different when you got off the plane and phoned your office.

While that's still possible, I'm not sure it's wise. Several people who read this in manuscript form told me you need a break about here. I now agree.

To this point we've really shaken up your thinking – challenged your understanding of, and approach to, your company. If you put this book down right now and didn't read another word, you'd never experience your business quite the same way again. That's true because *you're different already.*

That's why you need a break here. Think about what you've learned so far. Apply it to what's going on in your organization or business right now. Then shift your attention to something else. Let these concepts go subconscious.

Then, when you pick up this book again tomorrow, or on your return flight, if you're really on a plane, you'll dig into the rest of it fresh, and ready to go.

From here on, we'll take these concepts into action – into the real world – but in a very unique and powerful way.

Typically, management books give you skills which you can practice so you can become a better leader. If this were a normal management book, you'd read most of the rest of this book as "skills" to "learn."

But this *isn't* a normal management book. This isn't a book about *doing* something different at all. It's a book about *being* something different. About *being* your mission as a company or organization.

To convey those fresh ways of being, I'm going to present several new diagrams or models. If you kept reading now, they might appear to be over-whelming – too complex to absorb. Believe me, they aren't. I've watched summer hires working on county road crews grasp and apply them quickly. So I know they're worth the investment of your energy, your power, to understand them totally. As we go, I'll urge you to "fit them on like a favorite old sweater" so you can make them totally your own.

So what follows suggests ways to *be*, not things to *do*. Therefore, you'll need to be fresh to approach the models and concepts for their simplicity, not complexity. When you do, you'll grasp their significance immediately, and begin to use them quickly.

Enjoy your break. We'll begin again when you're ready.

CHAPTER 11

Why Companies Get Off Track

Welcome back. As I said, don't let the surface complexity of the next diagram put you off. It looks busy, but it's fundamentally simple, and it is critically important.

This representation was initially developed by Frank Burns and Linda Nelson for the Army coming out of the Vietnam war. It was literally the "theory" behind the Army's brilliant "Be all that you can be" mission in the late 1970's. Burns and Nelson published a version of it several years ago[4] that's well worth exploring.

The left column lists several attributes we often use to describe features of organizations. The remaining four columns describe each of those attributes from four different contexts: Reactive, Responsive, Purposed, and Authentic.

Look at the attributes under the Responsive context. Don't they describe the sort of organization you've worked hard to create? Isn't this the company most of us want? Of course it is. We all work to create an action planning, problem solving, goal setting, team building, successful-right-now company.

---

[4] Frank Burns and Linda Nelson, "High Performance Programming: A Framework for Transforming Organizations" *In Transforming Work: A Collection of Organizational Transformation*, ed. John Adams. Miles River Press, 1984.

Courageous Leadership

Context: Attribute:	Reactive	Responsive	Purposed	Authentic
Leadership	Enforce	Encourage/ Persuade	Mission	Holistic
Manage- ment	Fix Blame	Super- vision	Coach	Navigation
Intention	Avoid Pain	Rewards	Contribute	Fulfillment
Planning	Justifi- cation	Strategic/ Action	Commit- ment	Evolution
Structure	Frag- mented	Team	Alignment	Virtual
Change	Punish	Problem Solving	Self- Adjusting	Actuali- zation
Communi- cation	Force Feed	Feed Back	Dialogue	Improvi- sation
Orientation	Past	Present	Inclusive	Un- bounded

Luckily, every now and then, we get there. We achieve that kind of organization. But what happens as soon as we turn our back, or quit giving it our total attention?

Your answer is probably described by the words in the Reactive column. When things get out of hand, we tend to get serious about leading or managing. We start to enforce rules and policies with greater rigor. We get to the bottom of problems, find the culprits and forcefully correct their behavior. People become much more cautious, take fewer risks and justify their actions by the past. Cliques develop, barriers are raised, territories are claimed and turf is protected. You find yourself more and more in direct charge, giving more explicit and direct orders. Face it: you become autocratic, maybe even dictatorial.

We've all been in this kind of organization and we haven't liked it very much. How did it happen? Two key reasons:

First, in the Responsive context, we thought we had it handled. It was real, it was working, we had done what we set out to do. This was a *good* company. When we reach that level, we tend to think it will go on autopilot from there. It won't.

Second, even though you may not want to admit it, the company's success is dependent on your direct, personal leadership, and perhaps a few others. Some *one* keeps things on track by encouraging, supervising, rewarding, planning, resolving and feeding back.

In short, the structure is good, and is in place. But people are conforming to that structure; they're not putting forth their full creativity, and generating or innovating their own success and future.

You can't achieve the Responsive context and just maintain. You're either going forward, or you're going back. When you don't recognize what forward is, you have no choice but to fall back into the Reactive context.

Before we go any further, let's get one thing clear. While none of us wants to spend much time in the Reactive context, there's nothing wrong with the Responsive context. We need these skills early in our career. They are the structures and resources every organization uses.

But the tendency, when we drift back to the Reactive context, is to think we have to relearn Responsive skills, to get retrained. While perhaps temporarily useful or motivating, a lot of resources routinely are wasted retraining people in what they already know. That effort usually doesn't add to our repertoire.

Having said that, let's move on. What *is* beyond what you've worked so hard to achieve? What's beyond the Responsive context?

Look at the description of the attributes in the Purposed context. This is the context for companies which will take advantage of the insights in this book.

First, put your ego on the shelf. You're no longer in charge! The **mission** actually leads the company, not you. The core reason the company exists is what pulls everyone, including you, forward. That's why it's so critical to know exactly what that core mission is.

From here on you **coach**, not supervise. Your answers are not as valuable as your questions. Ask people what they intend to do. Tell stories on your-self – either successful results or unsuccessful. You can suggest ways people can increase their value and expertise, but in the end, they need to figure out how they can best contribute to being the mission.

People work for this company because they want to **contribute**, not just for the acknowledgment or rewards. Motivation is internal, not external. Motivation and success arise from the energy people bring to the mission.

Nothing really happens in this context until someone becomes **committed** to an outcome, regardless of the barriers or circumstances. One clear advantage: when commitment is present, results actually may be achieved before the plans have been developed.

Structures still will be important. Teams actually will form and disburse quickly, even effortlessly. The glue that holds people in this context together is not a specific framework, but their **alignment** with the mission. Teamwork can be taught in a classroom, but alignment occurs only when commitments are pooled to fulfill a mission.

Change is expected. Realities are **self-adjusting**. Using the momentum generated by the mission, it is frequently smarter to drop a problem that is 80% resolved, use what you've learned so far and begin working on an entire new situation. (We'll talk more about this possibility in Chapter 14.) After all, the point no longer is to be great problem solvers. The point is to be creating and fulfilling fresh possibilities from what this company *is*.

Communications are at the heart of this context. Virtually everything that is created here is done in a conversation, the conversation that is the mission. Since no one has the answer, the conversation is a **dialogue** about the current possibilities. What is said next – by anyone – is likely to be very important to realizing the mission.

A mission, remember, is not a goal. It's not something you are going toward. It just is. So the time orientation in this context is inclusive. Every orientation, past, present and future, is honored and acknowledged. The space this generates for mission led conversation is enormous.

So there you have a quick description of the Purposed context. The examples I've used throughout this book describe companies that lived in this context. Review the discussions about the Manufuturing mission, particularly in Chapters 3 and 5, and you'll gain a deeper understanding of this context in action. The only way it will truly work for *you*, however, is for you to take these skeleton notes and create the context in your company.

If the Purposed context is our focus, what's the fourth, Authentic, context? Frankly, my guess may be only slightly better than yours. But since we're either going forward, or we're falling back, there are no laurels to rest on in the Purposed context.

There is a context beyond the Purposed, I'm sure. The words in the fourth column are there as suggested guides. Let your experience and learning lead you into them, to explore for yourself. Over time, I'm sure we'll all be in more of a dialogue about what we've discovered.

CHAPTER 12

A Tool Guaranteed to Keep You On Track

Since it's so easy to fall back into the Reactive context, how can we be sure we're always on our mission? Let's return to the insight and wisdom of Bob Terry and study the matrix on the next page. It's an invaluable tool which will align and focus your energy.

With just a glance, it's easy to assume this is too complex to ever learn or integrate. Let me assure you again; it's not.

I watched the supervisor of a county highway department road crew use it perfectly to coach – and empower – a seventeen year old summer hire. The kid only wanted to rotate the Stop/Slow sign. That looked like a lot less work than wielding a shovel. Through dialogue with the supervisor and the use of this diagram, the youth recognized the limited value of his contribution. On the spot, he generated a greater commitment, and became a productive, energized employee.

How to Break Through Every Leadership Problem!

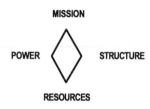

	MISSION	POWER	STRUCTURE	RESOURCES
mission	VISION	COMPELLING INTERESTS	GOALS AND POLICIES	LIFE EXPERIENCES
power	ENTITLE-MENTS	ACTS OF POWER	DECISION MAKING PROCESSES	SKILLS
structure	RATIONALE	INFORMAL POWER CHANNELS	ORGANIZA-TION CHART	TASKS
resources	LEGITIMACY	PRIORITIES	MECHANISMS	INVENTORY

Each axis of this matrix is labeled with mission, power, structure and resources. Read it by cross-referencing the horizontal axis with the vertical. Thus, the mission of mission (M,m) is "Vision." Your vision is fulfilled when you are the mission. It is the outcome of being the mission.

The next block to the right, the power of mission (P,m) is "Compelling Interests." These are the real reasons people get out of bed in the morning and come to work, the drives that internally motivate people to expend their energy.

People do what compels them. As an effective leader, you want to create opportunities for people to align their compelling interests with the company's mission. (If they can't do that, they probably won't be successful in your company. If you stand firmly in your mission, unaligned people will leave your company in short order.)

The block immediately below Vision deals with the mission of power (M,p). When you expend your energy toward achieving the vision you become "entitled" to fulfill many of your needs in this organization. Typical entitlements are a feeling of success, a sense of profound accomplishment and the right to be heard and respected. Each person perceives different entitlements. What is important is to understand that these entitlements are a direct result of people's contributions to the mission.

All people in the company are *always* doing powerful things. These are the "Activities of Power" (P,p). We use "...ing" words to describe this block: doing, creating, helping, achieving, producing or empowering are common and desirable ways energy is expended in organizations. Don't forget, however, *all* energy is spent on the job, including other "...ing" words like resisting, disrupting, delaying, sabotaging or shirking.

Actual activities of power are generated by each individual's perception of his or her own compelling interests, entitlements and vision. If the vision compelling you at work isn't your company's vision, your activities of power (what you're actually *doing*) probably will disrupt the organization more than contribute to its success. Unless you can align with it, you'll need to go. The same, of course, is true for everyone in your organization, and you'll probably discover it applies to your suppliers, even customers, as well.

While every box in the matrix is essential to your company's success, we want to focus on the mission and power boxes, rather than structure and resources. More often than not, people really *do* know how to deal with the structure and resources questions if their power is aligned with the mission. The reason most Responsive companies revert to Reactive is because people avoid facing the mission and power issues, then struggle to resolve intractable structure and resource questions instead.

That's the race track between structure and resources we described in Chapter 6. Use this matrix to avoid being trapped.

Leaders get trapped when they identify the wrong problem, then diligently set about "fixing" yet a different problem!

Use this matrix to pinpoint a problem, that is, put the problem in a box. Where did you put it? Wherever you put it, get ready for a shock. The *real* problem is *at least* one block *up*, and invariably we try to solve it one block *down*!

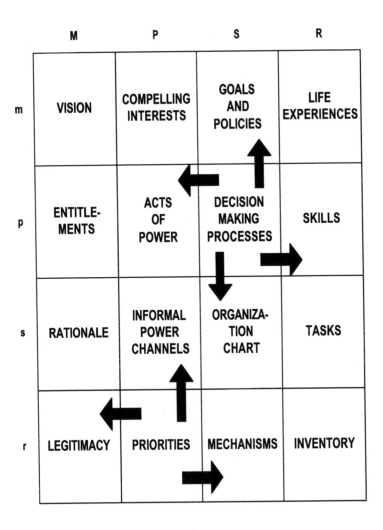

Look at the next example. Let's say you put your problem in the Decision Making Processes (S,p) block. The truth is, people generally make good decisions when their goals and policies are clear. If you tackle the problem one block up (S,m) by clarifying goals and objectives, better decisions will result. Instead, companies usually address this problem one block down (S,s), and attempt to resolve decision making problems by reorganizing (or firing or moving) the decision makers. Sound familiar? Have you done exactly that?

Since you ultimately want every issue, concern or contribution to fulfill the reason the company exists, you want energy focused toward the upper left-hand corner of the matrix, the Vision block.

Therefore, "up" or "down" work horizontally as well. "Up" is to the left, "down" is right. As represented in the diagram, suppose you decide you have a priority problem (P,r). As you can see, appropriate resolution comes by going one block up (left to M,r) and examining the "Legitimacy" of the priorities which are giving you trouble, based on the mission. (You could, of course, go geographically up and examine what's going on in the informal power channels – cliques and hidden agendas – that's impacting your priorities. That would be equally appropriate.)

Instead, we normally go one block down (right to S,r) and create a new mechanism for determining priorities. Typically, we establish a committee to review, revise or develop new priorities for the company. Again, sound familiar?

Ultimately, all questions and issues in your company must be addressed in the mission and power corners of the diamond model and matrix. If leaders don't move up and left consistently, they will constantly be driven down and right, eventually winding up in the "Inventory" block (R,r) every time.

Let me say that a different way: *Only after the mission and power questions are addressed can structure and resource issues be effectively resolved.*

This insight conflicts with most conventional wisdom about how organizations work. From the Responsive context, we assume that when an organization has a structure in place with stated goals, defined decision making processes, and a clear organization chart (all structure) – and when personnel have the required skills, understand their task, and do things with recognized priorities (all resources) – the organization will be effective.

Instead, this matrix demonstrates that *unless the organization has the top four left-hand blocks (mission and power) in place, the leader's best efforts to create and manage structures and resources begin to deteriorate almost immediately.*

Goals won't be met as expected, priorities will become contradictory, more skills will be needed, and soon everyone is calling for more money, more help or another reorganization.

The only certain way off this frustrating structure and resources race track is to break through to the compelling interests that determine the way energy is actually being spent in your company. That's what the road crew supervisor did with the summer-hire. He didn't need just a sign-turner in inventory. He needed this employee's compelling interest generating energy to efficiently pave roads. It worked.

If you still have questions about how to get started, Chapter 7 suggested ways to begin that dialogue.

CHAPTER 13

The Shocking Reality of Power

Now that you see the direct connection between mission and power – without an intervening structure – it's possible to look at power as you probably never have before.

Janet Hagberg has done a brilliant job of capturing and expressing the subtleties of power.[5] She identified six stages, or levels, of power in organizations. The concepts in this chapter are derived directly from her insights, and as with the other inspirations for this book, I encourage you to discover the full power of her contribution for yourself.

The first stage of power actually is **powerlessness**. We've all experienced this at one time or another. We're dependent on others, probably have low self-esteem, are uninformed or helpless and feel manipulated. At this stage we're motivated by fear.

While we can fall into a sense of powerlessness at a moment's notice, we hope we don't stay there often. Even so, all of us felt it the first day we began a new school, when we took our first job or when we were caught unprepared when we shouldn't have been.

---

[5] Hagberg, Janet O. *Real Power: Stages of Personal Power in Organizations*. (Revised) Sheffield Publishing Co., P.O. Box 359, Salem, WI 53168, (414) 843-2281, 1994.

Recognized Stages of Power in Organizations

	Power Stage:	Motivated By:	Manage By:
3	Achievement	Rewards	Monitoring
2	Association	Learning	Maneuvering
1	Powerless	Fear	Muscling

Unfortunately, some leaders and managers are at this stage much of the time. They lead by force. They manage by bullying and inspire fear in others. They say things like: "Are you questioning my authority?" "If you can't do this, I'll find someone who can!" It's not a pleasant stage, whether we're the boss or the recipient of the abuse.

The way to move beyond this stage is to build self-esteem, find allies, get support, develop skills, confront your fears and accept responsibility. Fear is really the only thing holding us back.

Once we move, the next stage is power by **association**. We're now feeling stronger because we're beginning to belong to something significant. We're motivated by learning: the ropes, the culture, the job, the politics.

Managers who live at this level maneuver. They deal. They inspire dependence. "Let's do lunch," is a conversation at this level. "If you do this for me, I'll remember it when you need something next time." Mutual back-scratching is a key tool for these leaders.

Some folks stay here forever. They gain their strength from what they belong to, or who they know or work for. Others move through this stage very rapidly. They're on their way to bigger and better things.

What holds people back in this stage is their lack of confidence and need for security. To move forward, develop your competencies, gain credentials, take risks, seek feedback, develop networks and find a mentor.

The third stage, power by **achievement**, is what we usually associate with bigger and better things. People at this stage have arrived. They are successful, expert, ambitious, egocentric, realistic, competitive, charismatic. They are motivated by rewards.

Managers monitor their subordinates effectively. They lead through personal persuasion. They inspire winning attitudes. These are the leaders who'll say, "Give me one reason why we can't do this, and I'll give you 20 why we can!" or "We have so much talent on this team, we can't fail. I'll see to that!"

Isn't this what we all shoot for? Isn't this the level of power, the level of success that's everyone's dream? Actually, for many people it is, and that's why power is such an elusive, even deceptive, commodity. Real power may not be what we think it is.

People at this level are actually stuck, and don't know it. They think they've arrived, and refuse to acknowledge the gnawing doubts all of us have at this stage: "Sure, I look cool, but inside I'm a bundle of fears. Am I as good as everyone seems to think I am? And even if I am, is this all there is to life and success?"

These are tough, important questions which many very successful leaders refuse to acknowledge and address. They have spent a lifetime building their egos and their careers. They are convinced, although they may not say it, that power is finite. There's really only so much to go around, and they have to hang on to what they've won. The rewards at this stage are very tangible, and they are attractive and desirable. And finally, corporations and society have never encouraged their leaders to express a lot of angst and self-doubt.

But if you want to taste real power – power that comes from who you are, not what the outside world bestows on you – you must move on. You must let go of your ego, recognize that power truly is infinite, discover and treasure intangible rewards and ignore those who discourage you.

Unrecognized Stages of Power in Organizations

Power Stage:		Motivated By:	Manage By:
6	Wisdom	Service	Musing
5	Purpose	Empowering	Moseying
4	Reflection	Process	Mentoring

In short, you must put your current success at risk, be willing to face yourself and your self-doubts. Look for others who have taken this step, and move into stage four: power by **reflection**.

Surprisingly, you haven't given up anything to take this risk. You're still strong, competent, expert. But now you're also more comfortable with your personal style. You're about to become skilled at mentoring, and beginning to demonstrate true leadership. You're motivated by discovering the underlying processes which generate human interaction.

Leaders at this stage are genuine mentors. They face their own demons, and are willing to share their experience with others. They model integrity. What you see is much closer to who they really are, than who they appeared to be when they were ego driven by success. These leaders inspire hope.

People at this stage don't give much thought to how they'll look. Instead, they ask, "What's the right thing to do?" and freely admit, "I don't have the answers, but I'm willing to explore the questions with you."

This tends to be an "in between" stage of power. People either retreat to known measures of success at stage three or lower, or they take their new awareness to the next level. What holds people back is their ego. If you can't leave that behind, you're not going to get much further.

Stage five is defined as power by **purpose**. Something bigger than the individual is pulling him or her forth. People at stage five are calm, accepting, confident, humble, visionary, spiritual, generously empowering. They no longer look one way on the outside and feel different on the inside.

People powered with purpose have encountered themselves head on, and now listen to their inner voice. Their reduced ego may look like naiveté or innocence. They may no longer fit the old corporate culture. They live to empower others to fulfill their purpose. These people manage by showing up. They mosey. They inspire love and service.

This is the level of power that can truly transform organizations, and it's available to anyone who contributes in the Purposed context described in Chapter 11.

There's a key secret in stages four and five which is critical to understanding the mission led organization. While much has been written and said about empowerment over the last decade, most efforts to empower haven't worked. In fact, empowerment has become a useless, even reviled buzzword. The truth is, in most cases, the detractors are right.

Leaders, who are at stage three themselves, try to empower people who are at stages one, two or three. That's not possible. At those stages we're too busy looking over our shoulder to see how others are accepting our actions to be genuinely empowered or empowering ourselves. In fact, there can be no genuine empowerment until you're willing to put your success at risk, and step into stage four. When you're willing to face yourself and your internal doubts, you create the possibility of becoming empowering.

Most leaders don't do that for two reasons. Some simply aren't willing to put their egos and success to that much risk. But the second reason is more legitimate.

It really doesn't make sense to genuinely empower people if there isn't a corporate purpose or mission to align them and pull them forth. You don't want to run a company of practicing self-doubters or out-of-control operators. And that's what you could have if there isn't a core, clear, compelling mission for your corporation.

Who I am, and what's really in me, matter a great deal when I'm contributing, committed and aligned in a Purposed context company. So while true empowerment hasn't happened much in companies, it's because most companies don't have a mission that can attract and align empowered people.

Before we leave this chapter, let's take a quick glimpse at the sixth stage: power by **wisdom**. When we're at level three or below, it's difficult for us to even realize this level exists.

People at this stage are comfortable with paradox, unafraid of death, ethical on a universal plane, and ultimately, once again, powerless. Mother Teresa is our clearest example, but people at this stage need not be old, and may not be famous. Your grandmother, a poet or a day-care administrator could be at level six in your world. Certainly, Ryan White, the 12 year old who died of AIDS a few years ago, was at level six. His composure and wisdom inspired us all.

Unfortunately, few people at this stage choose to work in companies or corporations; they have no aspirations to lead. They're motivated by service and manage – when they manage at all – by musing. That's unfortunate because this is the epitome of servant leadership. They have sources beyond most human experience. We feel their presence in our life. They tap our soul. Any company or organization would be blessed if more leaders were at this level.

Fortunately, this level of power in action has been captured on film in the documentary, "Mother Teresa." At the time, she was "CEO" of a "company" consisting of 1650 employees, plus 750 others in a 9-year training pipeline, at 230 locations, in 60 countries, on every continent. In spite of serving 42,000 clients in the worst of conditions, she refuses most donations of goods or equipment, and every donation of money! And you thought *you* had complex structures and not enough resources. Check it out at your neighborhood video store. It may be the best leadership training film of all time.

CHAPTER 14

More Tools for Letting the Mission Lead

I f most leaders never get beyond power stage three, what does it take to lead from stage four or five? Your first step is to review Chapters 11 and 12. They will support you as you develop yourself and your skills.

In this chapter we'll explore three more concepts which will help you create the space to get your ego out of the way, and let the mission lead. Each is somewhat counterintuitive, and they certainly contradict how we were raised to be in action and in control.

One of the most persistent models is that leaders and managers are problem solvers. We're taught to define the problem, describe what it will look like when the problem no longer exists, then close the gap between where we are and where we want to be – in other words, to solve the problem.

This figure describes a different possibility. The gap is where the action is. It's where all creativity, innovation and productivity occur. Why on earth would you want to close it?

Open...
Don't Close
...The Gap

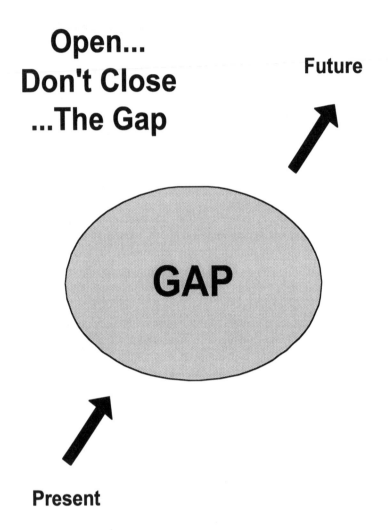

Future

GAP

Present

When you know why your company exists and are willing to put your success at risk, don't close the gap. Step into it with both feet. And encourage everyone else to jump in with you. Then, rather than closing or narrowing the gap, expand it! The orientation in a purpose driven organization, remember, is all inclusive, not just future oriented (see Chapter 11). Don't deny the past you've created. Expand the gap to include the past, the present and the future.

Mission led companies are constantly at risk because they remain in the gap. That's also the reason they are outrageously successful and productive.

How do you gather enough courage to routinely live in the gap? First, you need to recognize that the rules of the game have changed. You've read this, probably experienced it yourself, thousands of times in recent years.

The Old Organizational Contract

You pledge your loyalty to a company, and you belong. Because you belong ("we're a family in this company") you're trusted. When you belong and are trusted, you're safe and you're pretty well assured of a career.

That reality no longer exists. But many of us aren't very pleased with what seems to have replaced it. We're not pleased because it doesn't make any sense – from power stages one to three. It only begins to make sense and become desirable when we step into the gap that is power stage four.

The New Organizational Contract

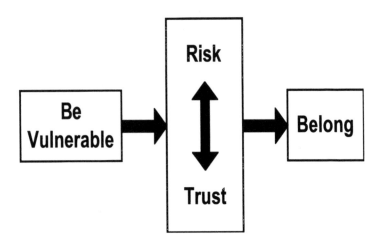

There is no guarantee any more that you will belong. The only security you have is to be vulnerable. It doesn't matter whether you're a new hire on your first job, or the CEO. When you're vulnerable, you have no choice but to take risks and trust yourself and others. That mutual trust and risk-taking are what creates results. One of those results is genuine belonging.

In short, if you want to belong to a mission led company today, you must put it all on the line, make a commitment to the mission, align your contribution with others and leap into the gap – all with no guarantees. While you don't have to do this to continue to draw a paycheck, don't kid yourself that you're being led by a compelling purpose. You're not. You're retaining your safety, and keeping your ego secure.

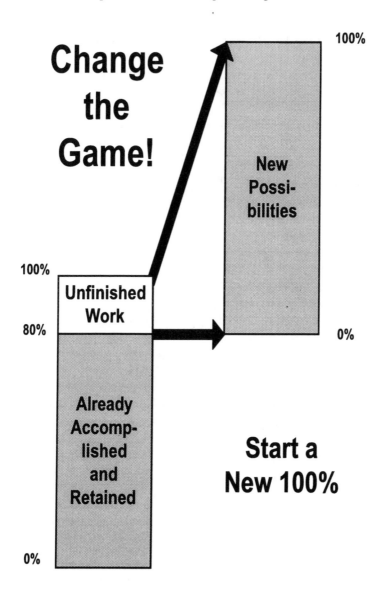

So here's another way to generate an entire new gap and to put all your success at risk.

Organizations which set goals and objectives typically make rapid progress immediately. In this illustration, let's assume you accomplish as much as 80% of what you set out to do.

Then things begin to get bogged down: expected resources don't materialize, key people leave the company, deadlines are missed. As good managers, we take a more personal interest. We get more involved. Pay more attention to the details. Monitor more often. The result: progress continues to be made, but at a much slower rate, at a much greater cost to us. It often takes as long to get from 80% to 83% as it did to get the first 80%; and the next percentage points come even more dearly.

What if you didn't do that? What if you captured what you'd achieved in the initial 80%, took it all with you, and created an entirely new gap – a new goal or objective – a new 100%?

Confident leaders on clear missions do exactly this. Their purpose is no longer to complete the goal. Their purpose is to fulfill the mission. These leaders are no longer attached to the plan. They are committed to the company being everything it can possibly be, without structural limitations.

Let your mission pull you into the vulnerable fourth stage of power. Open the gap wider, invite everyone in, create frequent new 100%s. You'll be glad you did!

CHAPTER 15

Make Tough Choices Easier

Confident leaders often get shaky when faced with ethical dilemmas. We've all heard (and usually subscribe to) the old adage "Don't do anything you wouldn't want to read about in tomorrow's paper." While that's useful, it certainly doesn't address all situations, and even if we do that, we may still be blind-sided by issues we didn't expect. That's exactly what happen to Kathy Lee Gifford when her clothing line was attacked for being manufactured by child labor in emerging countries.

The diagram in this chapter will take you beyond your current understanding of ethics, and give you a foundation to make tough choices easier in the future. By now you won't be surprised to learn that the source of this thinking is our friend and mentor, Bob Terry. As you have with his earlier concepts, get ready to discover subtleties of ethics you never dreamed existed.

In Chapter 11 you discovered that a model that looked complicated, actually wasn't. This model, too, is not difficult to comprehend. Terry simply adds two new levels to the Mission, Power, Structure, Resources ladder you're familiar with: Meaning on the top, and Existence on the bottom. Then he plots those six levels against three other columns.

When you read Terry's book, *Authentic Leadership*, you'll get the full richness of his thinking, but for now, it's enough to define Existence as simply the "stuff" that becomes Resources when it's included in, and used by, an organization. Let's define Meaning as the profound, usually spiritual, force that pulls your company's mission into being, and keeps it alive.

The center of the three columns gives each level of Ethics a specific name. The left, or Metaphor, column describes a typical way we might express that ethic in everyday conversations. The right column, Rules Out, denotes a specific undesirable condition that is eliminated if that particular ethic is in place or being observed.

Approach the chart from the bottom, or Existence level, and work your way up as we discuss each ethic in turn.

We probably all agree with the first level, Dwelling. Life is a gift. Everyone is entitled to their space and time. Genocide is wrong, not just unethical. But this is precisely the ethic we struggle with when we consider our stand on capital punishment, ethnic warfare and abortion. Lives conflict at an ethical level. Each player in these situations is addressing this ethic from their perspective. Tough choices have to be made. How do we decide?

We move up a level. We make freedom the arbiter. All of life's possibilities should be available to everyone. America was founded on the belief in individual freedom, an ethic at the heart of traditional conservative politics. Rugged individualism. Land of equal opportunity. Less government, less regulation, less control is best.

Authentic Ethics

	Metaphor	Ethic	Rules Out
Meaning	**Art** (Improvisation)	**Responsibility**	**Abdication**
Mission	**Life is a Journey** (Not destination - It's the trip)	**Love** (As caring. Pay attention to well being of others)	**Indifference** (Breaks the revenge cycle)
Power	**Life is Full Expression**	**Empowerment** (Full participation)	**Oppression**
Structure	**Life is a Body** (The benevolent community)	**Justice** (Equality: give due; Equity: proportionality; Imagination)	**Double Standards**
Resources	**Life is a Market Place** (Life is a machine)	**Freedom** (Individual possibilities)	**Discrimination**
Existence	**Life is a Gift**	**Dwelling** (Sacred place, space, time)	**Genocide**

That worked until we could no longer ethically rationalize slavery, and we went to war with each other over our ethical freedoms. The struggle has continued in many other forms through the years, but, thankfully, this country is comfortable enough addressing the issues of freedom that we have come a long way toward reducing, if not fully eliminating, discrimination.

How did we learn to balance those individual freedoms? We moved up a level to justice. As school children, many of us were raised on the standard that "This is a nation of laws, not of men." Individuals can't just do anything they please. Fairness is ultimately arbitrated in legislatures and courts. Since life is inherently *not* fair, it takes a benevolent community to ensure justice, the traditional liberal position. Regulate and legislate justice. If we get it right, and behave ethically at this level, we'll rule out double standards.

Again, while significant progress has been made, we're beginning to recognize the limitation of legislation and government in regulating ethical choices. What is just beginning to become evident is that our standard measures of justice, equity and equality, aren't enough. Even when we pay attention to justice, some groups or individuals still feel oppressed. Our legal and legislative systems have not dealt well with those charges. The Rodney King verdicts and aftermath amply demonstrated that. Justice, we're learning, requires imaginative new solutions.

As a mission-led, power-aware leader, you're in the perfect position to move beyond this dilemma. There will be no end to oppression until everyone is fully empowered to be who they are. Not just with access to resources, which is the individual freedom ethic, but with full participation, full expression, with all the vulnerability, risk and trust that involves (see Chapter 14).

This level of ethical choice is possible in your company because you, and everyone else, knows why the company exists. Your mission is clear, so people's compelling interests can be fully expressed and aligned with the mission.

If they can't express themselves in this organization, they're quickly aware of the misalignment and easily move on. They are not oppressed, confined or restricted by other individuals, rules or regulations.

Ethical decisions at the mission level essentially are questions of love. Your mission is *now*, it is not something you're going toward. Your mission is the journey your company is. It is the way your company expresses its love. When you participate in your company's mission, you can't be indifferent. You must constantly measure your alignment and the results being produced with the mission.

Most people assume that the opposite of love is hate. Actually those two are very closely related emotions. We go from one to the other in an instant. The *real* opposite of love is indifference; we just don't care. In a mission lead company you can't be indifferent.

Organizations which express the love they are, break out of past cycles of revenge and conflict. What matters is everyone *being* the mission, not who wins or even what's fair.

When you accept that level of ethical choice, you begin to realize the full impact of your decision. Regardless of any sentiment, any political persuasion, any law or regulation, in the end, you are responsible. You cannot abdicate your responsibility. There are probably no guidelines. You have to make it up as you go along; you have to improvise.

To illustrate this dynamic, let's return to Kathy Lee Gifford. Set all your personal opinions of the woman aside for the moment. It doesn't matter whether you like her, enjoy her television personality or have any other opinion of her. She faced a significant public ethical dilemma, and demonstrated most of the stages in this model.

Gifford's persona is one of someone who respects life. She would agree that life is a gift and would be appalled at killing and suffering.

She's also an astute business person, who has capitalized on that persona to endorse a very successful line of clothing. She would agree life is a market place, and that we are all entitled to have an equal opportunity.

Even if she hadn't been a successful woman in television and in business, with strong alliances and partnerships in both, she has been known as a supporter of causes, including child welfare. She would agree that life is a body and we are a community in it together.

To this point, things went very well for Gifford. Then her world crashed. Charges were made of child laborers producing her clothes in appalling conditions. She was accused of condoning double standards. What did she do?

Quite naturally, she reacted at the justice level, and took some of her accusers to court. But she didn't stop there. She pushed on up the ethical ladder. She took direct action to find out for herself what was really happening. She visited the factories, talked to the workers, testified before congress. She vulnerably participated fully, and did not tolerate or condone oppression, at significant financial, perhaps even personal, risk.

I don't know how she'd say it, but the mission Gifford *is* was evident in the love she expressed for the workers. She refused to hide in the existing laws, and deliberately tackled the indifference that was rampant in the industry.

In the end, Gifford took full responsibility. She did not abdicate. And she made it up as she went along; she improvised. Often that didn't look very pretty or polished. She didn't care. She was clear about who she was and she was fully responsible.

Gifford always would have considered herself an ethical person. Most of us probably would have agreed. She wouldn't have intentionally "done anything she wouldn't have wanted to see in tomorrow's newspaper." But that's exactly what happened. She was blind-sided. And she responded with the full range of ethical responsibility. In the end, she will be stronger, and probably richer, for it.

You may be blind-sided at any time. You can't prepare for every possibility. But now you know how to respond if it happens. And you even have an

Stages of Power and Ethics

	Power Stage	Ethic	Rules Out
Meaning	Wisdom	Responsibility	Abdication
Mission	Purpose	Love	Indifference
Power	Reflection	Empowerment	Oppression
Structure	Achievement	Justice	Double Standards
Resources	Association	Freedom	Discrimination
Existence	Powerless	Dwelling	Genocide

advantage Kathy Lee Gifford didn't have. You can live at the upper levels of ethics all the time.

Now capitalize on your awareness of higher stages of power. Notice how Hagberg's six power stages blend with Terry's ethical choices. You want your employees empowered. Invite them not just to participate, but to express their compelling interests fully, within your company's mission. Eliminate any possibility of oppression. Express your mission as the love it is. Be indifferent to nothing. And finally, make it up as you go along. Your mission is not a science, it's an art. You're responsible and you cannot ever abdicate that responsibility.

CHAPTER 16

Find Structures That Support Missions

So far this book has focused primarily on the Mission and Power corners of the diamond, and dealt very little with Structure and Resources. Why? Two fundamental reasons.

Since you are as successful as you are, you already know a vast amount about designing, building, maintaining and even changing structures needed for organizations. That's what you've learned over the years on the job. Most leaders are genuine experts in putting structures in place.

Secondly, and surprisingly, resources are not a real problem. As I said in Chapter 5, *when you're absolutely clear about your mission, you have all the resources you'll ever need!* I know that sounds like nonsense, but clarify and live your mission, and you'll discover it's absolutely true. I don't know why it's true. It just is.

Even with your experience, there are some fresh ways to approach structures and resources which can be very useful. To get your creativity going, here are a couple of examples that worked in mission led situations.

Let's deal with missing or inadequate resources first. At one point in my Navy career, I was assigned to train all the Navy's organizational development specialists. The Navy had been using internally trained consultants for several years, with considerable effectiveness and success. Their success, however, was generally the result of their ingenuity and experience once they were on the job, not the quality of the education they received as students at the school that trained them.

The problem was a Navy policy that consultants could not do two tours of duty as organizational development specialists. That meant that successful, field-experienced consultants rarely, if ever, returned to the school as instructors. Instead, the instructors were people who had just been through the basic course, then turned their hat around, and instantly became part of the faculty.

What you would expect to happen happened. New instructors were given a lesson plan that was supposed to last for an hour of instruction. Without any personal experience to flesh the lesson plan out, the instructor would complete the entire plan in 10 or 15 minutes and panic. Students knew the instructors were in over their heads, and all the disruptive behavior you would expect routinely occurred.

Rather than challenge the policy, which had been attempted several times without avail, I agreed to create an effective faculty within this system. The only way to do that was to create a mission that would pull all of us, staff and students, forward. That mission was "Creating Consultants Together."

In other words, it was no longer the job of the inexperienced instructor to pull the students forth. They really didn't have much to teach. Instead, everyone was now equally responsible, students and instructors. Everyone knew the limitations of the policy, and it was no longer a valid factor. Lesson plans were guides to discussions and co-creation, not lectures to be delivered. Everyone's experience, student and instructor, constantly was tapped. You were expected to contribute to your own, and to each other's development.

It worked. Discoveries were common. Hidden talents flourished. Creativity, ingenuity, innovation and huge insights emerged from every corner. Graduates left with much more depth and expertise than from any previous classes.

We knew we had succeeded in creating a structure from a unique mission when instructors could go into the classroom with the same one-hour lesson plan. But this time, rather than be through it to panic in 15 minutes, they'd frequently get to the end of the hour and realized they'd only covered a third of the lesson! There was support to spare. Confident in their contribution and certain of the students growth during that hour, the physical plan was only useful, not essential. It was never again a useless crutch.

Where are you slim on resources? Who have you made responsible for that situation? Are they really floundering because they think it all depends on them? Consider creating a mission for that situation. What resources would appear; what structures would emerge, if the mission were some variation of "creating the outcome together?" When you're clear about the mission, you have all the resources you'll ever need.

Now let me share an example of a structure that empowered and produced outstanding results.

Action plans, with goals, objectives, steps and re-sponsible persons are common structures in most organizations. In Chapter 14 we learned to abandon worn out plans quickly, but this conversation's about using them while they're effective structures.

Have you ever been asked to itemize the lessons learned from an experience, trip or project? Those slips of paper or formal reports go into the system, but do they produce action? What comes of your insights and contribution? All too often they disappear, never to be heard of again, until the same problem recurs on the next trip or during the next project.

One organization was in that trap. Lessons learned were not used. Rather than continue to throw insights down a black hole, the group leader formulated an action plan, a structure, in an unusual fashion.

Calling all the members of his team into a conference room, the leader asked them to say anything they wanted to say about the experience that had just taken place. The group literally covered the walls with newsprint in about 45 minutes. The leader thanked them, said he would get back to them and excused them.

From that information, over the next few days, the leader shaped all that information into about eight clear objective statements. Then he invited the group back to the room. (It *was* an invitation. He did not require attendance. Most members chose to come to this and later sessions.)

"If we achieved these objectives, would we successfully benefit from the insights we discovered during the experience?" he asked. With minor discussion, rewording and perhaps the addition or subtraction of an objective or two, the group agreed, again, in less than an hour.

Saying, "Thanks, I'll call you again," the leader let them get back to work. Next he drafted goal statements he believed would achieve the agreed objectives and reassembled the group.

This meeting took even less time, primarily because the participants were learning to trust the leader and believed their concerns were being heard and addressed.

Finally, the leader devised action steps and assigned appropriate responsibilities and reasonable timelines – mostly without asking the people he was assigning responsibilities to (many of them even outside his sphere of influence) if they concurred or agreed. Then he called his group together one last time.

"What needs to be added or changed?" Again, minor adjustments, but the meeting, which resulted in agreement on what turned out to be a half-inch thick action plan, was quickly over.

The final plan was printed and distributed to everyone who had been assigned an action responsibility. Remember, for many of those people assigned actions, this was the first time they were even aware the plan was being built.

The leader went back to his office, put his feet on his desk and waited for the phone to ring. It did.

Typically, the caller would start with a comment like, "Wow, this is great! We should have done

this months ago." Then they would get to their concerns: "You've got me scheduled to provide this by
the first of October. I appreciate the problem but
there's no way I could have it done by then."

"Ouch," the leader would reply. "I should have
checked with you more thoroughly. When could you
have it ready?"

"I could guarantee it by the middle of November," the caller might respond, "but that may screw
up others in the pipeline."

"Listen," the leader reassures. "If you'll promise it by the 15th of November, I'll talk to everyone
else, and make sure no one gets bent out of shape.
Will that work?"

"You bet," closes the caller. "Thanks for getting this cleared up."

Stage three power behavior? Probably. But it
was generated from stage four and five energy and
alignment. While there were many phone calls like
this, since no one, including the leader, owned this
particular structure, it could be reshaped constantly
to support and empower others to produce what
was needed.

As a practice, the leader published a status
report on this plan that went to everyone every
couple of weeks. It reported changes in deadlines,
acknowledged completed actions and ultimately
became such a living document that new objectives
and goals were added on the fly.

This was a structure that worked. It took far
fewer resources than normal action planning sessions and was inordinately successful because it
was inherently fluid.

There's one important fact not to overlook here. This entire structure was created because the leader and his particular team were frustrated by an existing lessons learned structure that did not work.

At the original meeting – the one where the group covered the walls with newsprint – the leader admitted he had an outrageous, blatantly selfish, mission: "Make Our Job Easier!"

The initial reaction was what you'd expect: mild shock, laughter, a little uneasiness: "Can we really do that?" Once beyond that reaction, everyone in the group left the room aligned with that mission. They were ready for this aspect of their job to be easier.

In the end, even the people who were assigned actions without prior input or knowledge usually aligned with the mission. The leader openly used the mission in his phone conversations, saying something like, "Look, I want to be sure this will make your job easier. Will it?" Invariably the caller's response was, yes, it would help to have whatever the issue was resolved by the deadline.

So where do you look for structures that will support you as you spend your energy being a mission? Anywhere at all. But more often than not, you'll literally make them up.

Where do you look for the resources you need to be the mission. Anywhere at all. But more often than not they're right in front of you or just over your shoulder. When you're clear about who you are – clear about your mission – the resources you need to fulfill it will show up and the structures that work will literally suggest themselves.

CHAPTER 17

Don't Get Cocky –
And What to Do When You Do!

When you're clear about the mission of your company or organization, miracles happen. It's not necessarily *easy* to align an existing organization with a mission, but it *is* simple. You declare the mission, and spend your energy *being* that mission. You invite everyone else who is involved to do the same. If they can't or won't, they aren't a part of that mission, and they won't be around very long. If they enroll, they align the interests which compel them and contribute their power and expertise to being the mission. It's that simple.

Problems appear from at least two directions: many successful leaders don't understand why it's working (CEOs haven't a clue, remember?) or, leaders abandon their mission without replacing it.

Many leaders of very successful, mission led companies never realize why it's working! They are simply unaware of the dynamics, the fact that they are *being* a mission, not just building an organization. They think results are coming because they cleverly created structures that work and they are prudently using available resources. They're doing that, of course, but that's not their real focus. Their real, unrecognized focus is *being* the mission.

A classic example of this sort of success is Steve Jobs and the team that built the Macintosh computer. They may not have stated it exactly this way, but they existed to create a "warm, fuzzy computer." They decided what that was, generated resources, created supportive structures and aligned their energies to fulfill that mission. It worked like a champ and their experience is almost a textbook case of a mission led organization.

So why do I say they didn't know what they were doing? After the Macintosh was created, Jobs lost control of Apple and eventually was booted out. His response was to gather many of the key Macintosh development team members and start a new company from scratch. His new company, NeXT, was intended to build a computer which would serve college level students and staff.

By now he was cocky about his own and his team's ability. He didn't clarify the mission. Even worse, he didn't talk about the mission nearly as much as he talked about building a company. This is tantamount to saying the mission of NeXT is to be a *company*. And, Jobs would add, one that was better than Apple.

Who cares? No one wanted a Macintosh until Macintoshes existed. The team creating the Macintosh *was* the mission. While we may have been fascinated by its story, no one really cared that Apple existed as a company. It was the *mission* – Macintosh – that really mattered.

While we may find him interesting, no one really cares whether Jobs creates another company. However, the product, the collegiate computer as reason to exist, might have got our attention. When the team focused on the structure of the company, not the mission, they moved quickly to the Reactive context. They missed virtually every deadline, ran out of resources, argued among themselves and blamed each other. Ultimately, the NeXT computer was almost two years behind schedule when introduced, and never became a significant factor in the market place.

Jobs gets full credit for pulling it off at Macintosh, but flunks when it comes to understanding why it worked. *You* won't be caught without that knowledge. You know the reason your company exists and let that reason, that mission, not your ego, lead.

The second kind of problem occurs when you literally abandon your mission due to circumstances you feel are beyond your control. We began this book with Domino's Pizza, so we'll close with it as well.

Over the years, several people were seriously injured or killed in traffic accidents involving Domino's delivery vehicles. Staying true to its mission of "A Pizza in 30 Minutes," Domino's resolved these incidents either in arbitration or through the courts. The accidents, however, were a blot on Domino's reputation and a genuine concern for everyone involved.

Finally, Domino's founder, Tom Monaghan, decided these repercussions couldn't continue. He formally announced that Domino's, while it would still be fast, no longer would promise to deliver a pizza in 30 minutes. We can all understand his rationale for making this decision, but it literally will kill his company and he doesn't know it.

Monaghan, in his announcement, shifted the emphasis from speed (the mission) to taste (a previously unused feature). I hate to be the one who tells him, but (and I don't care if Domino's pizzas are now actually the best tasting pizzas on the planet) no one *believes* Domino's pizzas taste good! We never have bought them for their taste and we never will. Frankly, Monaghan should know this already. In the past he's tried some advertising campaigns which stressed Domino's taste. Remember "Avoid the Noid?" What did that have to do with Domino's mission?

Okay, so the moral and legal pressure just became too much and Monaghan, prudently, he felt, dropped the mission. Was that his only choice in the situation? Not at all.

If Monaghan truly believed that Domino's did, and always would, exist to deliver a pizza in 30 minutes or less, he had at least one other option. *Rather than abandon his mission, he could have abandoned his structures and resources.*

He could have closed down and sold off all the existing store fronts. Let all those teenage daredevils who drive the beat up old VW delivery vehicles go. Used the money gained from these actions to purchase mobile vans equipped with cellular phones, refrigerators and microwave ovens. Then he could have staffed each of those vans with an overly cautious driver/order taker/delivery person and one cook.

By placing those vans strategically in neighborhoods, they'd practically be cruising your block when you called in your order! Then Domino's could market these changes with a new ad: "A Pizza in TWENTY minutes!" Beat *that*, Pizza Hut!

In short, if you *are* your mission, you have all the resources you'll ever need and anything is possible. Domino's may be in business for many years. Lots of companies with unclear or nonexistence missions are. But Domino's won't have it as easy as they have in the past. If I can get a good pizza in roughly the same amount of time that Domino's might get its pizza to me, I'll probably opt for the good pizza more often than not.

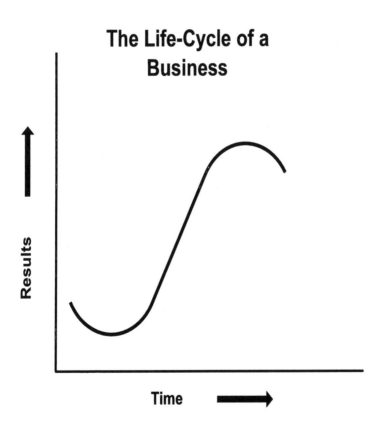

The Life-Cycle of a Business

Virtually every organization experiences an "S" curve like the one illustrated here. There's an initial dip as things get going, then, hopefully, a lengthy upward trend. Most leaders accept the dip in the beginning and pray the upswing goes on forever. It doesn't. There comes a time when the curve loses momentum and ultimately degenerates. Most businesses today which are more than a couple of years old are struggling at the top of their current curve, simply trying to prolong the inevitable.

After reading this book, you don't have to do that. You know you can't maintain status quo. Why wait for the acceleration to decrease? Take the risk to create a new 100% while you're still accelerating. Start a new "S" curve right now.

Sure, you'll experience a brand new dip; you'll lose some ground. But look what you accomplish once you're through that. The curve goes well above anything possible before.

This is what it looks like when you put your success at risk and vulnerably apply the context of this book. Initially it will confuse you and others. There will be a dip in productivity and performance. You'll have doubts about whether it was a good idea and wonder why you even consider going on.

Honor those concerns, but *be* your mission. The result will be an entirely new "S" curve.

You now have the basics to re-ignite your business. Get on with it.

Discover the singular, solitary, core, bone-deep reason your company exists. Courageously examine how you and your people are actually spending your energy. Is it aligned with, and fulfilling, your company's reason to be?

Apply what you've discovered in this book in your situation or organization. You'll lead with infinitely more confidence, ease and certainty. I guarantee it. As I promised in the Introduction, if you apply these contexts and you don't believe you've doubled your confidence, I'll personally refund the money you invested in this book. The form to fax requesting your refund is at the back of the book.

Call me regardless. Let me know your successes and the concerns or barriers you encounter. Who knows? Maybe your experience will be highlighted in my next book for confident leaders.

About the Author

Dick Barnett is a speaker, consultant and coach to successful business leaders.

A graduate of Northwestern University, he began discovering and applying these concepts during a 22 year career as an officer in the Navy. Following years at sea – including extensive service in Vietnam river and coastal waters – he spent the last third of that career as an organizational development specialist. Before retiring as a Commander in 1984, he was responsible for designing the curriculum and creating the Navy's organizational development specialists, as well as training every Navy leadership instructor.

Since then, hundreds of business owners and leaders have worked with Dick and Bill Kutz, co-founder of Barnett & Kutz, Inc., discovering and applying the context he's outlined in this book. Clients as varied as "Mom and Pop" small businesses to large corporations like Nike, Tektronix, Kaiser Permanente, California Closets, Epson, Special Olympics, Subway Sandwiches, American Medical Response, VTech and Nordstrom have taken their businesses to new levels of performance and productivity applying these insights.

Dick's articles appear regularly in magazines like *Consultant Report, Directions* and *Free Enterprise Journal.* He's interviewed for publications like the *Business Journal* and *Investor's Business Daily*, and he speaks internationally on this topic.

You'll learn how to benefit from Barnett & Kutz, Inc. consulting and coaching services, or schedule Dick to present a program for your organization, by calling (503) 629-5210.

Re-Ignite Your Business Accomplishment Report

Wow, Dick. This really worked! I've Re-Ignited My Business and I want to share my results with you and other readers. Our mission is _____

_____ ,
and here's what we've accomplished since we let it lead our company: _____

_____

_____

_____

You may publish these comments as a testimonial in future editions or marketing materials. ❑ No

Contact me. I'd love to tell you more about my experience with this context. ❑ No

Name: _____ Company: _____

Address: _____

Telephone: _____ Fax: _____

Signed: _____ Date: _____

I want to share this book with other colleagues. Please send _____ more copies at $15.95 each (includes Shipping and Handling). My Visa/Mastercard number is

_____ Exp. Date _____

Fax this form to (503) 645-7099, or mail it to: Dick Barnett, Barnett & Kutz, Inc., Cornell Oaks Corporate Center, 15455 NW Greenbrier Pkwy, Suite 210, Beaverton, OR 97006-5700.

Re-Ignite Your Business
Results Guarantee

Sorry, Dick. It didn't work for me, so I'm taking you up on your guarantee. I've read and reread **Re-Ignite Your Business,** defined the following mission _____, and applied your coaching to my situation. I just wasn't able to let my mission lead and our performance hasn't improved as you promised.

The biggest problem I encountered was: _____

_____

_____

The thing that worked best for me was: _____

_____

_____

But that wasn't enough to justify the cost of your book. Please refund the $_____ I paid for it to me:

Name: _____ Company: _____

Address: _____

Telephone:_____ Fax: _____

Signed:_____ Date: _____

Fax this form to (503) 645-7099, or mail it to: Dick Barnett, Barnett & Kutz, Inc., Cornell Oaks Corporate Center, 15455 NW Greenbrier Pkwy, Suite 210, Beaverton, OR 97006-5700.